EDINBURGH GRAVEYARD GUIDE

MICHAEL T R B TURNBULL

SCOTTISH CULTURAL PRESS
www.scottishbooks.com

For Finlay Michael

First published by St Andrew Press
This revised and updated edition
published in 2006 by

Scottish Cultural Press
Unit 6, Newbattle Abbey Business Park
Newbattle Road, Dalkeith EH22 3LJ Scotland
Tel: +44 (0)131 660 6366 • Fax: +44 (0)870 285 4846
Email: info@scottishbooks.com
website: **www.scottishbooks.com**

British Library Cataloguing in Publication Data
A catalogue record for this book is available
from the British Library

ISBN-10: 1 898218 16 1
ISBN-13: 978 1 898218 16 6

Design Concept by Mark Blackadder

Printed and **bound** by
Athenæum Press Ltd, Gateshead, Tyne & Wear

Contents

Introduction

Graveyards are a fascinating gateway into the extraordinarily rich lives of the men and women who have found themselves, by accident or design, in the capital city of Scotland.

There are those such as the five Scottish American Civil War veterans who died overseas and whose bodies were brought back to their native land. There are the unfortunate passers-through suddenly struck down – such as the scientist Julius von Yellin, from Munich, who was in Edinburgh only to give a lecture. There are those who, like the tragic-comic poet William McGonagall, were born and died in the city. Then there are the publicly executed criminals and, finally, the Royal babies, many of whom scarcely saw the light of day . . .

A word of caution to the curious visitor – some of the graveyards of Edinburgh present formidable obstacles, such as 15-feet high Giant Hogweed or physical threats from only too real human spectres lurking in the ruins of long-forgotten graves. For safety's sake, never walk alone!

Location of Graveyards

(with approximate dates of foundation where known)

1 Edinburgh Castle	Royal Mile (Castlehill)
2 Greyfriars (1562)	Candlemaker Row
3 St Giles (1140)	Royal Mile (High Street)
4 Canongate (1691)	Royal Mile (Canongate)
5 Holyrood Abbey (1128)	Royal Mile (Canongate)
6 Old Calton (1718)	Waterloo Place
7 New Calton (1817)	Regent Road
8 Dean (1845)	Dean Path

Edinburgh Graveyards (a map of the city is advisable for those burial grounds outwith the city centre)

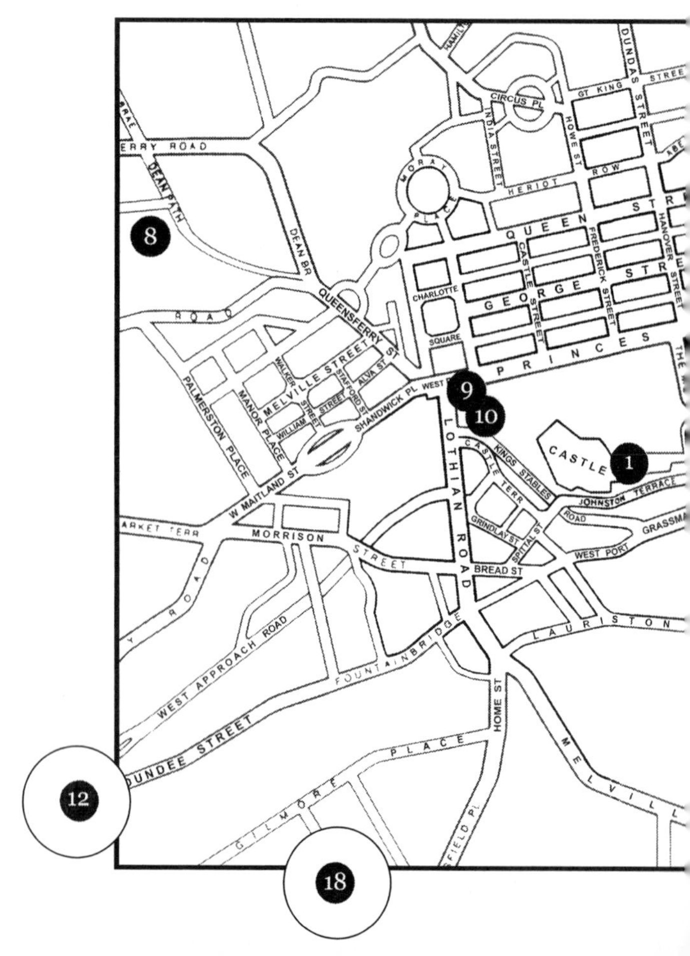

9 St John's (1818)	Lothian Road / Princes Street
10 St Cuthbert's (1127)	Lothian Road
11 Buccleuch (1756)	Charles Street
12 Colinton (1650)	Dell Road
13 Grange (1846)	Beaufort Road
14 Warriston (1842)	Warriston Gardens
15 Piershill (1887)	Portobello Road
16 Rosebank (1846)	Pilrig Street
17 Mount Vernon (1895)	Mount Vernon Road
18 Morningside (1878)	Morningside Drive
19 Restalrig	South Restalrig Road
20 Craigentinny	Craigentinny Crescent
21 Tron Kirk (1747)	Royal Mile (High Street)

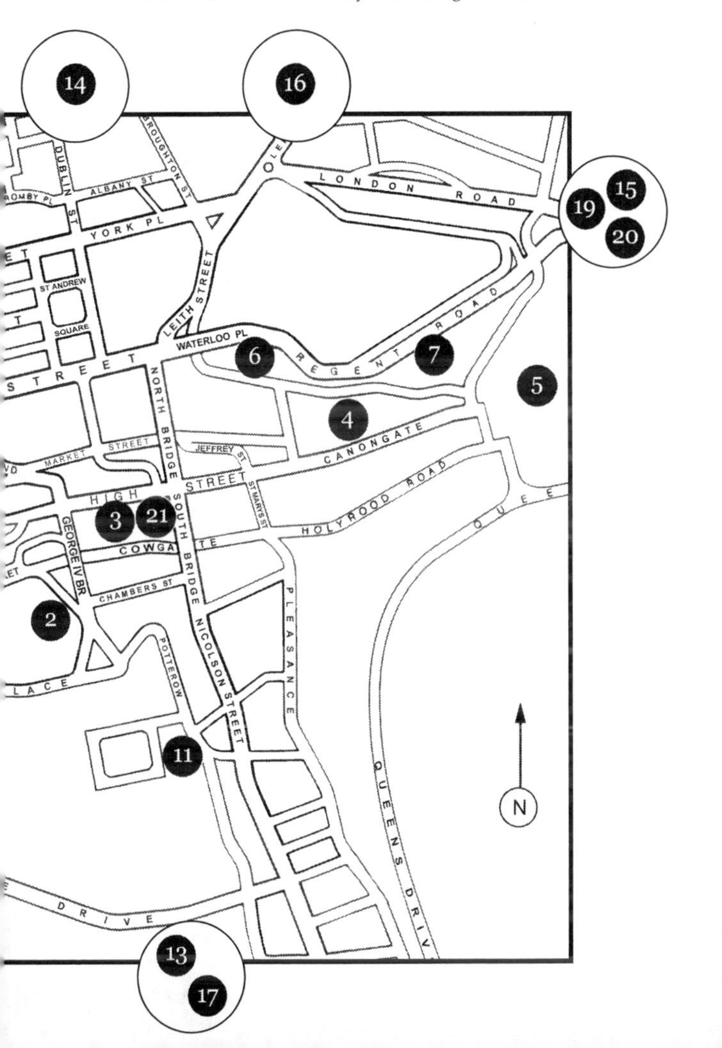

EDINBURGH CASTLE

Location – Castle Rock

The wings of death hover over the Castle. It started perhaps in the mists of the Dark Ages when it is said that the old 'Maiden Castle' (as it was once known) held the graves of many young girls, dead before their prime.

Although the Castle was occupied since the Bronze Age, only a few burials have been found there. One such body is thought to have been that of the young Earl of Douglas, who was lured to his death in the banqueting hall . . .

The 'Black Dinner' of November 1440 was an act of extreme savagery. Eighteen-year-old William, 6th Earl of Douglas, and his young brother David were invited to dinner at the Castle by King James II.

Edinburgh Castle

Dog Cemetery

During the meal a black bull's head was carried to the table: this was the signal for the Earl and his brother to be seized (in spite of the protests and tears of the young King), taken to the Castlehill and immediately executed for treason.

The injustice and cruelty of the Black Dinner were condemned in an old ballad:

Edinburgh Castle, toune and toure,
God grant thou sink for sinne!
And that even for the black dinoir
Earl Douglas got therein.

In addition, a number of muscular skeletons (probably part of Cromwell's army) were discovered in the late 20th century.

The only formal cemetery in the Castle is the **[1] DOG CEMETERY** for army dogs. Among the many well-loved pets and regimental mascots is Pat VC (*d.*1887) who followed the 72nd Highlanders. Pat saved his master, a colour-sergeant, during the Afghan War. When his master was attacked by an Afghan soldier, Pat bit the assailant's calf. For his bravery, Pat was awarded the Dickin Medal.

During the Crimean War, Bob of the Scots Fusiliers chased cannonballs and often burned his nose on a hot one. He was awarded a special silver medal but was run over by a butcher's cart outside Buckingham Palace. Later he was stuffed and put in a glass case in a place of honour.

On the Castle Esplanade many a soldier died in attack or in defence – from the siege of Donaldbane (1093) to the invasion of the Earl of Hereford in 1544. However, at the foot of the Esplanade (on the north side) is the **[2] WITCHES FOUNTAIN** which commemorates the popular hysteria and judicial cruelty which flourished for several centuries all over Europe.

Designed by artist John Duncan for the architect Sir Patrick Geddes in 1894 and erected in 1912, this stylish bronze drinking fountain commemorates the 300 supposed 'witches' who were tied at the stake, strangled and then burnt to ashes on the Castlehill between 1492 and 1722.

The purpose of the drinking-fountain is to record the fact that not all witches worked for evil. The serene head is Hygiea, goddess of health, and the serpent is the symbol of Aesculapius, god of medicine (still honoured by doctors today). Though the foxglove produces poisonous digitalis, it is also a thing of beauty, and the 'evil eye' can be kept at bay by the hands of healing. Through the cleansing fire on the centre panel passed black magicians and also the

Witches Fountain

North Berwick witches

well-intentioned practitioners of homeopathic medicine, as well as elderly or bewildered persons wrongly judged to be malevolent.

It was King James VI and I (himself born at Edinburgh Castle) who fuelled popular paranoia about witches in his book *Daemonologie* (1597). Seven years before, the King suspected that witches had conjured up violent storms while he was sailing back to Scotland from Denmark.

In the trial that followed, men and women confessed under torture that 200 witches had sailed in sieves from Leith to North Berwick and then danced round the churchyard in the presence of the Devil.

Suspects were tortured by being kept awake, tormented with thumb-screws and by crushing their legs in the buits (wooden wedges). One woman claimed she had hung a black toad upside down for three days and then collected the venom in an oyster shell.

Janet Horne, burnt at the stake in 1722, was the last witch to be executed in Scotland – although the persecution of so-called 'witches' lasted for another 30 years in mainland Europe. In all, it is thought that over 4,500 'witches' were killed in Scotland.

On the Esplanade there is only one formal grave – that of **[3]** Ensign **CHARLES EWART** (1769-1846) (at the top right corner of the Castle Esplanade, before you cross the draw-bridge).

A block of grey Norwegian granite placed there in 1938 by the Royal Scots Greys, marks the grave, as does the original carved plaque set in the ground behind.

More than 600 men took part in the battle of Waterloo (1815). In the charge of the Union Brigade, they came to within 200 yards of Napoleon himself.

Sergeant Ewart (later commissioned to Ensign) of the Royal North British Dragoons, described his capture of the Imperial Eagle standard of the French 45th Regiment of Infantry, from which the eagle cap badge of the Royal Scots Dragoon Guards (Carabiniers and Greys) is taken: 'It was in the first charge, about 11 o'clock, I took the Eagle from the enemy. He and I had a hard contest for it . . . then I cut him from chin upwards, which went right through his teeth.

'Next I was attacked by a foot soldier who, after firing at me, charged me with his bayonet, but he very soon lost his combat, for I parried him and cut him down through the head, so that finished the contest for the Eagle,

Imperial Eagle

Ensign Ewart

which I took into Brussels midst the acclamation of all who saw it.'

Ensign Ewart was born in the Scottish Borders but died in bed in Manchester at the age of 77. In 1937 his burial place was found in a contractor's yard in Salford and his remains re-interred in the Castle Esplanade.

The Castle holds a number of articles associated with Ensign Ewart: the sword he carried at Waterloo; his Waterloo medal; the watch he bought in Paris; his silver snuff-box and the coatee he wore as a member of the Veteran Battalion.

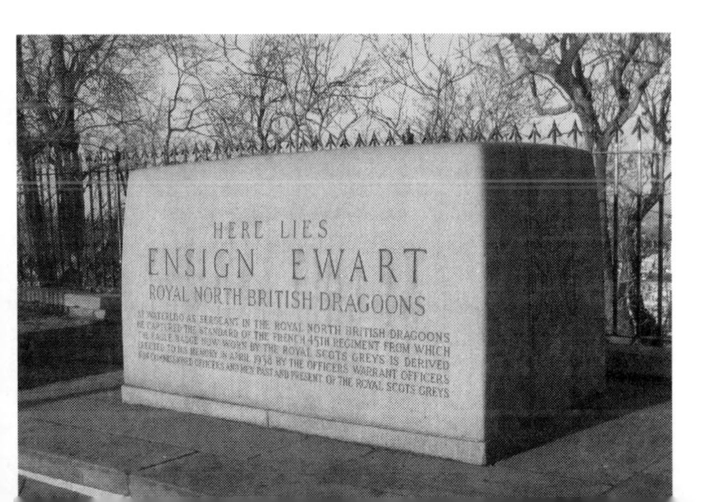

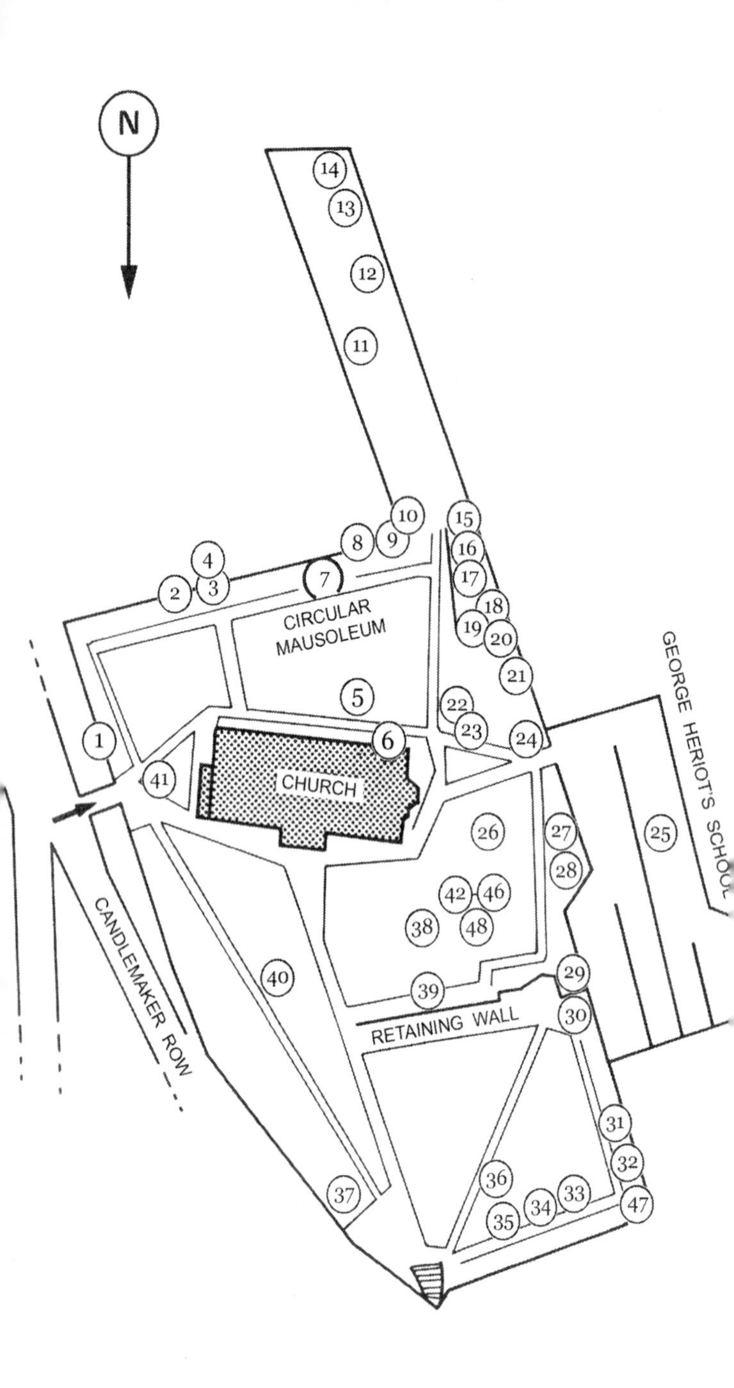

Greyfriars Churchyard

Location – Candlemaker Row

2

GREYFRIARS

Your first glimpse of Greyfriars Kirk will probably be behind the bronze statue of the faithful Skye terrier 'Greyfriars Bobby' ('from life just before his death') at the junction of Chambers Street, George IV Bridge and Candlemaker Row. He sits patiently on his granite fountain, the drinking-well, unhappily, now quite dry.

Facing you is Greyfriars Bobby's Bar with a penny-farthing bicycle fastened to its rugged stone front and the profile of the wee dog in black above the door.

Go into the churchyard round the left side of Greyfriars Bobby's Bar, up uneven cobbles, under an old lantern fixture high overhead. Already a sixth sense warns you that this is a place of ancient mystery.

Where you stand was once the site of the monastery and garden of the Franciscan Order (the 'Grey Friars' wore a brown habit: in those days the colour brown was classed as a shade of grey). The Franciscans first came to Edinburgh in 1447 as medical missionaries treating the needs of the poor. At the Reformation they escaped to the Continent.

In 1562, the garden of the Greyfriars was given to the Town by Mary Queen of Scots as an overflow cemetery to relieve the overcrowding in the churchyard of St Giles, the original parish church of Edinburgh. Between then and 1900 nearly 100,000 people were buried in the churchyard.

Hugo Arnot, writing in 1778, records that 'the graves are so crowded upon each other that the sextons frequently cannot avoid, in opening a ripe grave, encroaching upon one not fit to be touched. The whole presents a scene equally nauseous and unwholesome.'

To add to the overcrowding, when St Giles was being restored in 1879, several tons of human bones from unmarked graves in the middle of the church were removed and reverently re-interred at Greyfriars.

You may be surprised to hear that the location of many graves is unknown. In 1603 the Town Council ordered all gravestones to be removed: thus the earlier graves in Greyfriars were marked only with numbered wooden posts.

Since burial records were not kept until 1658, the exact location of the graves of a number of famous people is not known and probably never will be . . .

The Kirk is a giant barn shooting into the sky. On the east wall, facing you, the bulging rib-cage of a skeleton prances, swinging a scythe and holding the *Book of Destiny* (you can almost hear the skull cackling). Sharp surgical knives and scissors hang on each side, tied with bows. Ignore the quivering skeleton if you can. Turn immediately to your left past the noticeboard that glitters with the names of the famous dead. If you listen carefully, you can almost hear a low murmur of many muffled voices from beneath your feet.

John Mylne

The first grave to the left is the imposing monument to **[1] JOHN MYLNE** (1611-67), the sixth Royal Master Mason in his family. Above, a heraldic shield is gripped by two beefy men. A dragon roars below. Under it a contented winged soul spreads its feathers.

Mylne was the fourth John to be a Master Mason from a family that served seven successive kings. Ironically, not one of the Mylnes was ever knighted for his services to Scotland.

John Mylne designed the Tron Kirk and built part of Heriot's School (where a fine statue of him presides over the quadrangle). Mylne was not only a builder, he also represented Edinburgh in the Scottish Parliament.

The carved cloth bearing the main inscription – '*Great Artisan grave Senator; John Milne*' – is framed by the ferocious heads of monsters (perhaps from his nightmares?) Two ornate pillars on either side trumpet epitaphs and commemorative verse.

According to the inscriptions, Mylne was remarkably handsome, honest, pious and respected everywhere. But the picture you get from his tomb tells a totally different story: skulls, an hour-glass and crossed torches burning upside down speak of the fear and pain of death which must have haunted Mylne and all the people of Edinburgh in his day.

Shaking off the shiver tingling up and down your spine, walk slowly up the path as it swings right. At the sixth windswept walled grave is a burnished plaque dedicated to the memory of **[2]** Sir **ROBERT SIBBALD** (1641-1722), Physician to Charles II and founder of Edinburgh's Royal College of Physicians, King's Geographer in Scotland and first Professor of Medicine at the University of Edinburgh.

The good doctor, however, was a bit accident-prone. On one occasion he was coming out of the close at his home, setting off to see a sick child, when his spurs locked together and, slipping on the wet cobbles, he tottered forward and fell headfirst against the side of the stair. On another occasion he was accidentally hit over the head by a golfer making a wild stroke on Leith Links.

But accidents did not prevent Robert Sibbald from continuing his tireless work for the world of medicine. He helped found what is now the Royal Botanic Garden when he planted one of Edinburgh's first public gardens for medicinal herbs – on the site of the present Waverley Station booking office.

In Sibbald's day the world of learning was smaller and it was possible for one man to have a diversity of jobs and achieve much in one lifetime. The influence of this pioneering Scottish doctor (who had studied his medicine in Holland and France) was enormous. Today his place of burial is open to the skies.

Tread warily past the next walled grave to the ten-pillared stone canopy over the last resting place of **[3]** Commissary **CLEMENT LITTLE** (*d.*1580) and his brother **[4]** Lord Provost **WILLIAM LITTLE** (*d.*1601).

They were two of the three founders of Edinburgh University. Clement Little, an advocate, left 300 books as a generous foundation for the University Library.

Four grim women (noses missing and one headless) stand on guard over the roof. The story once went round that they were four cruel daughters who poisoned their father (now to be seen resting nonchalantly in his tomb). This was a colourful and widely believed way of explaining the eerie-looking monument. The mysterious female figures on the roof seem to threaten the man lying helpless below.

Clement Little

In reality, the disturbing statues are far from evil. They are the virtues Justice, Mercy, Faith, Love: the good qualities for which the Little brothers wanted to be remembered.

Justice has her eyes blindfolded. One hand grips a sword, the other holds weighing scales. Another figure wears a laurel crown and clenches squirming snakes in her hand. The weather has not treated them kindly, but they stand erect as silent sentinels on the roof.

Under this canopy a plump, badly dressed man (William Little) casually rests his head by one elbow on a tasselled cushion, as if taking a nap after supper.

Now leave the safety of the path for a moment. Turn right towards two heavy black iron 'mortsafes' (security cages) beside the church, designed to stop those vultures of the night – the grave-robbers (or 'Resurrectionists') looking for fresh corpses to sell for medical research.

Getting bodies for teaching anatomy was always difficult. As early as 1505 the Town Council allowed the College of Surgeons the body of one criminal each year. But this was not nearly enough – anatomical dissection was seasonal; it could only be practised in the winter when bodies could be kept cold. In the summer putrefaction quickly set in.

In February 1678, four gypsies called Shaw (a father and three sons) were hanged and thrown together into a pit in the churchyard. On the following morning the body of the youngest son, aged 16, was seen to be missing. Some thought he might have revived under the shallow pile of earth, having been hanged last and first cut down.

But it was strongly suspected that his body had been stolen by a surgeon.

Over the next 30 years Greyfriars (the chief burial ground in Edinburgh at the time) saw more and more graves robbed by surgeons' apprentices. They worked with great secrecy. In those days no one but a grave-robber would dare to go into a churchyard after sunset.

By 1694 the corpses of those who died in the correction house, or the bodies of foundlings who died at the breast, were handed over to surgeons for dissection. At the Royal College of Surgeons today you can still see a skeleton and dissection by Professor Alexander Monro Primus and Dr Archibald Pitcairne, both of whom are buried in Greyfriars.

Outside Britain the Resurrectionists were almost unknown. In other countries a reasonable supply of bodies was available legally.

In May 1711, the Royal College of Surgeons protested that 'of late there has been a violation of sepulchres in the Greyfriars Churchyard by some who most unchristianly have been stealing, or at least attempting to carry away, the bodies of the dead out of their graves'.

Ten years later the College of Surgeons ordered the insertion of a clause of indenture for apprentices, forbidding them to take part in the theft of bodies from graves.

But very little changed and in 1725 the people of Edinburgh gathered in the streets to protest at

Dr Robert Knox, the anatomist (1791-1862)

the offensive trade in human flesh. They went to Professor Monro's School of Anatomy and smashed the windows, putting the fear of death into the doctors and their apprentices.

In 1742 the body of Alexander Baxter (who had been buried in Greyfriars) was found in a house next to the shop of a surgeon called Martin Eccles. The Portsburgh drum was seized and beaten through the Cowgate. The interior of Eccles' shop was demolished, windows in the homes of other surgeons were smashed and the riot was put down only with great difficulty. Eccles and some of his apprentices were taken to court, charged with the offence of being accessory to the lifting of bodies, but the case had to be abandoned because of lack of evidence.

Sir Robert Christison gives a detailed account of the grave-robbers' techniques: 'The time chosen in the dark winter nights was for the town churchyards from six to eight o'clock, at which hour the churchyard watch was set and the city police also commenced their night rounds.

'A hole was dug down to the coffin only where the head lay – a canvas sheet being stretched around to receive the earth and to prevent any of it spoiling the smooth uniformity of the grass.

'The digging was done with short flat, dagger-shaped implements of wood, to avoid the clicking of iron striking stones.

'On reaching the coffin two broad iron hooks under the lid pulled forcibly up

Catchpole, once used by Edinburgh police

with a rope broke off a sufficient portion of the lid to allow the body to be dragged out. Sacking was heaped over the whole to deaden the sound of cracking wood. The body was stripped of the grave-clothes which were scrupulously buried again. It was secured in a sack and the surface of the ground as carefully restored to its original condition – which was not difficult as the grass over a fresh-filled grave always shows sign of recent disturbance. The whole process could be completed in an hour.'

Between the two mortsafes in the churchyard is a large flat gravestone set into the grass. Here lies **[5]** Lord President **DUNCAN FORBES** of Culloden (1685-1747), a dragon on the helmet of his coat of arms poised above three muzzled bears and unicorns.

Forbes was born on the family estate at Culloden near Inverness. As a law student he was a fierce drinker and gambler – he and his brother were known as the greatest boozers in the North. At his home – Culloden House – casks of claret were emptied by the pailful and the massive dining table was stained red with wine.

When Forbes' mother died, the funeral party was so intoxicated that they arrived at the graveside without the body!

But Forbes became a Member of Parliament, and in 1737 Lord President of the Court of Session. He began his career by making the Scottish legal system more efficient.

Lord President Duncan Forbes, by Roubiliac, in Parliament House

During the Jacobite Rebellion Forbes sided with the Hanoverian King George, but after the battle of Culloden he saw to it that the prisoners were tried not in England (where they would have little chance of a fair trial) but in Scotland. He opposed any overruling of the Scottish Court of Session by the House of Lords in cases of forfeiture of estates, as this would have been against the Treaty of Union. He objected to the Disarming Act of 1716 which would have made it unlawful for Highlanders to carry weapons of any kind.

After the Porteous Riots, when the English Parliament was determined to strip Edinburgh's Lord Provost of his office, abolish the Town Guard and knock down the Netherbow Port, Duncan Forbes, a true patriot, stood firm for the honour of his country.

So powerful and respected did he become that he was known as 'King Duncan', but he was also called 'one of the greatest men that Scotland bred, as a judge, a patriot and a Christian'.

Proceed with caution towards the end section of the church wall in front of you. Between the last two buttresses are 11 memorial stones set high up into the church wall. In the middle is one to the cheery poet and publisher **[6] ALLAN RAMSAY** (1686-1758) who is buried in the churchyard in an unknown location:

Tho' here you're buried, worthy ALLAN,
We'll ne'er forget you, canty Callan,
For while your Soul lives in the Sky,
Your GENTLE SHEPHERD ne'er can die.

Ramsay, Lanarkshire-born, served his apprenticeship as a wigmaker. He was a tiny, chubby little man with an ugly face, but full of fun and amusing conversation.

In 1712 he opened his own wig shop and founded the Easy Club. His next business was at the 'sign of the Mercury' (showing a winged messenger) on the sunny side of the High Street. Six years later he published his first book of poems and then in 1724 his *Tea Table Miscellany*, a collection of Scots songs and ballads.

Ramsay then set up a bookshop at the end of the ramshackle Luckenbooths beside St Giles and opened a lending library – it was the first one in Britain.

The first regular professional theatre in Edinburgh was his next project. This opened in 1736, but closed down by the bigoted magistrates soon after as they disapproved of public theatres, which they thought were irreverent and encouraged civil disobedience.

His final home was an octagonal villa on the north side of the Castlehill, the 'goose-pie' as it was affectionately known (from its shape and from Ramsay's amiable character).

When the Jacobites captured Edinburgh in 1745, Ramsay, a secret Jacobite sympathiser, moved out of Edinburgh, and his house was used by Prince Charlie's men to take pot-shots at the Castle.

Now turn away from the church to the imposing but gloomy domed monument with a mysterious urn on its roof (beside the tomb of the Little brothers). Walk slowly

Allan Ramsay

over the grass towards it between two menacing green obelisks.

Already there is a sense of faint unease in the air, for this is the tomb of **[7]** Sir **GEORGE MACKENZIE** (1636-91), better known as 'Bluidy Mackenzie', the hanging judge, a man both hated and respected.

Mackenzie boasted that he had never lost a case for the King, but he also worked to prevent the cruel and senseless persecution of so-called 'witches'.

His opinion of heretics was that 'it fares with them as with tops, which, as long as they are scourged they stay upright and run'. He had a violent temper, an insolent manner and a cutting tongue. In court he once threatened to pull out a Covenanter's tongue with a pair of pincers.

Yet Mackenzie had other sides to his character – he wrote a pioneering legal work (*The Institutes of the Law of Scotland*) as well as one of Scotland's earliest novels, *Aretina; or, the serious romance* (1660). He also gifted 1,500 books to the Advocates Library (which he founded in 1680). This formed the basis of the present National Library of Scotland.

His monument is gloomy but, in architectural terms, finely-designed. Delicate flowering columns separate alcoves shaped like scallop shells. These are the traditional badges worn by pilgrims to St James' shrine at Compostella, Spain. They tell us that, for Mackenzie, life was a long journey towards God and ultimate forgiveness.

In the alcove to the right, you can see where forgotten schoolboys long ago carved letters into the stone. The solid oak door to the tomb is pierced by two rusty iron grilles, fragile as lace. Peep through them into the shadowy heart of the tomb and you see more scallops inside, scooped out of the stone. Rattle the lock and shout the 'dare' of the George Heriot's schoolboys over the centuries: *Lift the sneck and draw the bar: Bluidy Mackenzie, come out if ye daur!*

Today there is no longer a sneck and a bar – only a stout padlock.

There is also a happy story about the Mackenzie mausoleum. About 1780 a young man called Hay, the son of a stabler in the Grassmarket, was in the North Bridge prison under sentence of death for burglary. He managed to escape and reached Greyfriars churchyard. An accomplice had given him a key to the Mackenzie tomb which of course had a reputation for being haunted by the ghost of Sir George (today's well-known 'Mackenzie poltergeist').

Hay had been a schoolboy at George Heriot's nearby and his hiding-place was kept secret by the schoolboys who fed him faithfully for six weeks until he was able to escape overseas.

In 1897 a Clerk of Police, J W Weston, who inspected the interior of the Mackenzie tomb, recorded that he 'saw and touched the actual hand of Sir George Mackenzie'.

The next grave along has only the engraved black letters that record the name of **[8] PATRICK MILLER** of Dalswinton (1731-1815). It is

'Bluidy Mackenzie's' tomb

open to the elements and unmarked but for the carving above the lintel.

Miller, Glasgow-born, was a director of the Bank of Scotland, but his hobby was experimenting with machinery. A shareholder in the Carron Ironworks, he helped improve the quality of their cannons and is said to have been involved in the invention of the deadly carronade.

Much of his spare time was spent in Leith improving the way ships were designed and built. He believed that a steam-engine could be used to power boats and in 1788 tried out a pioneering steam-powered vessel near his own estate on Dalswinton Loch in Ayrshire. Among the passengers were the portrait painter Alexander Nasmyth and the poet Robert Burns (a local tenant).

Walk on with a fresh step to the final wall monument to your left. It is to members of

Covenanters Prison

the great theatrical Siddons family – **[9] HENRY SIDDONS** (1774-1815) and his wife **[10] HARRIOT** (1783-1844).

Henry Siddons was the eldest son of the famous actress Sarah Siddons (1755-1831). He appeared at Covent Garden for the first time in the play 'Integrity' in 1801 and eight years later took over Edinburgh's Theatre Royal in Shakespeare Square (later the site of the General Post Office at the east end of Princes Street) until his death. His wife was a fine actress and a beautiful woman. After her husband's death, she ran the theatre, its greatest success being Sir Walter Scott's *Rob Roy* presented in 1819. When King George IV visited Edinburgh in 1822 Mrs Siddons played Diana Vernon. She retired in 1830.

Now you approach gates marked 'The Covenanters Prison'. For some time this was thought to have been the place where 1200 defeated Covenanters were held in 1679, but the actual site is known to have been on the Forrest Road side of the churchyard on a piece of land now built over. The ground beyond the locked gates was not in fact used for burials until 1705. If the gate is locked, the key can be obtained by prior arrangement with the city burial ground or church authorities.

James Hutton

Go through the gate. At the eighth plot on the left, halfway down, walk through a gate in a low wall armed with railings. Facing you, below a higgledy-piggledy red brick wall, is a simple white marble plaque to **[11] JAMES HUTTON** (1726-97) known as the 'Father of Modern Geology'.

James Hutton

Living in Edinburgh all his life, Hutton was fascinated by the tortured, twisted rocks of the ancient volcano still visible in the Castle Rock, and most of all in Arthur's Seat and Salisbury Crags jutting out of the earth high above the Queen's Park.

The love of Hutton's life was chemistry. He began as an apprentice in a lawyer's office, but instead of getting on with the drudgery of copying legal papers, he amazed and amused his fellow-apprentices with spectacular chemical experiments.

Hutton soon gave up his job and instead went to study medicine in Edinburgh, Paris and Holland, graduating as a doctor in 1749.

Then Hutton was left a small property in Berwickshire. He now began to experiment with new methods of farming and set up a business making salt from coal-soot. He went to England to look at advanced farming methods and consequently became equally fascinated by soil and rock formations.

In 1785 he presented his *Theory of the Earth* to the Royal Society of Edinburgh. His theory came as a bombshell; challenging the accepted view that the earth had been formed by the action of the sea. Hutton showed that it was principally volcanic activity which had shaped the earth's crust, and he used detailed studies of the rock formations at Edinburgh's Salisbury Crags to back up his theory.

For all that he was a scientific revolutionary Hutton was a very quiet man. He never married and lived with his three sisters. He ate very little and never drank wine, yet there is an amusing story about him and his friend Dr Joseph Black.

One day the two learned men were arguing about food. Why did people eat creatures like oysters which crawled upon the sea-bed but refused to touch snails which crawled on dry land? So they ordered a dozen snails. Although neither liked the look or smell of the snails, neither wanted to back down. With a gulp the two doctors swallowed the snails, their faces squirming, their stomachs churning.

Black gave way first – 'Doctor, don't you think they taste a little – a very little queer?' 'Damned queer!' Hutton replied 'Tak them awa, take them awa!'

A little further down on the opposite side of the path lies Hutton's friend and contemporary **[12] JOSEPH BLACK** (1728-99), Professor of Chemistry.

Black was born in Bordeaux where his father was a wine merchant, but he was educated in Belfast and then trained as a doctor in Glasgow.

In 1750 Black came to Edinburgh where he was the first to identify carbonic acid and then returned to Glasgow as Professor of Chemistry to discover the phenomenon known as latent heat. This opened the way for James Watt to improve the steam-engine. In 1766 Black was appointed a Professor at Edinburgh.

Joseph Black

He was a calm, unexcitable man. Any stress or strain would result in him spitting blood. But his easy temperament and pleasant smile meant that he had a lot of friends. Like Dr Hutton he never married.

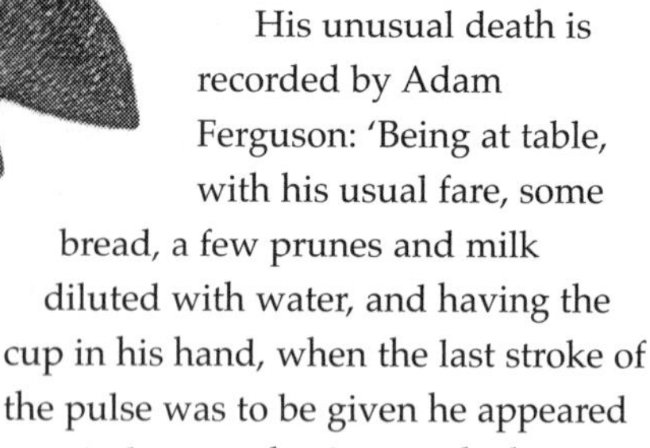

Lord Monboddo

His unusual death is recorded by Adam Ferguson: 'Being at table, with his usual fare, some bread, a few prunes and milk diluted with water, and having the cup in his hand, when the last stroke of the pulse was to be given he appeared to have set it down on his knees which were joined together and in the action expired without spilling a drop.'

His 20 foot high monument is almost identical to that of Adam Smith in the Canongate churchyard. Fine strips of stone radiate from the centre – beams of light from a shining mind. On each side are the intertwined snakes of the medical profession, while in the centre a bearded head forms the keystone of the arch – this is not a portrait of Dr Black but a symbol of his powerful, wide-ranging mind.

Further down on the same side, in the third burial-plot from the end, is the grave of **[13]** James Burnett, **LORD MONBODDO** (1714-99), an unmarked grave within the family enclosure of Patrick Grant, Lord Elchies.

Born in Kincardineshire, Monboddo was educated at Aberdeen, Edinburgh and in Holland. On 7 September 1736, the day of the Porteous Riots, he returned to Edinburgh, where he was nearly arrested for being involved in the mob.

A glittering career as an advocate followed and in 1767 he was made a Lord of Session. As a young man Monboddo loved the theatre and dancing, particularly the minuet (which he danced dressed in a white velvet suit).

Later in his life, however, he was to be described as 'rather like an old stuffed monkey'. Monboddo, for his time, had rather progressive ideas about healthy living. Summer and winter he would get up early and take a cold bath. Before going to bed at night he used to cover himself in a cream made of rosewater, olive oil, aromatic spirit and Venetian soap.

Monboddo also had a military career. At the battle of Sherrifmuir he was on horseback when he came upon an English officer who had been stunned after falling off his horse. Monboddo rode up to him and the officer gallantly said, 'Sir, I am your prisoner.'

'No,' answered Monboddo (seeing other English troops approaching), 'I am *your* prisoner.' 'If that is so,' said the officer, 'get off your horse and I will protect you' – and Monboddo was escorted to safety.

Monboddo was best known for his six volumes of *The Origin and Progress of Language* (1773-92) which suggest that the human race was descended from orang-utangs and that children were born with tails. To prove such ideas (which in his lifetime brought him a great deal of ridicule) he pestered midwives to allow him to watch women giving birth. In this respect he can be seen as a forerunner of Charles Darwin (Darwin himself was partly trained at Edinburgh University).

Buried beside Lord Monboddo is his daughter **[14] ELIZA BURNETT** (1766-90) – one of the most attractive and intelligent women of her day.

When Robert Burns first met her at one of Lord Monboddo's famous suppers at the Monboddo home in the Canongate, he wrote: *'Fair Burnett strikes the adoring eye, Heav'n's beauties on my fancy shine.'*

But, in spite of many offers of marriage, Miss Burnett chose to look after her father. She died from consumption aged 24. Burns composed her epitaph: *'Thy form and mind, sweet maid, can I forget? In richest ore the brightest jewel set!'*

Returning to the main part of the churchyard, first on your left is the restored mausoleum of the Adam family, with its bust of **[15] WILLIAM ADAM** (1689-1748), affectionately known to his family as 'Old Stone and Lime'. The monument is the work of three of his sons – Robert (aged 19), James (17) and William (9).

Not far from Greyfriars at the east end of what today is Chambers Street was the town house of the Adam family (they were originally from Kirkcaldy in Fife). Across the South Bridge is Infirmary Street, once the location of the first Royal Infirmary which William built in 1747. After the demolition of the building, the richly-carved Drummond Scrolls and four pillars were re-erected in Redford Road in 1884 by a far-sighted MP for Leith, Robert Macfie; while the original ornate gates can still be seen not far away in Drummond Street. The statue of George II as a Roman emperor which adorned an alcove at the front of

William Adam

Principal Robertson

the old building stood for many years outside what was the second Royal Infirmary.

Other buildings worked on by William Adam include Hopetoun House, The Drum (at Gilmerton), the Town House (Dundee) and Robert Gordon's College (Aberdeen).

William Adam was a many-sided man, setting up breweries, introducing strong ale (*barley-bree*) into Scotland and opening Dutch-tile factories which roofed half of eastern Scotland.

Standing beside the Adam monument is the almost equally resplendent tomb of **[16]** Principal **WILLIAM ROBERTSON** (1721-93), chiselled ridges of stone shining out over its arch in laserbeams of light.

Robertson was a minister, a historian and Principal of Edinburgh University. He was partly responsible for what became Old College and was a founder member of the Royal Society of Edinburgh, a meeting place for the finest minds in Scotland. The son of a minister, Robertson was a distinguished preacher and a leading Moderate at the General Assembly. He was also the author of several important works of history such as *History of Scotland* (1759), *History of Charles V* (1769) and *History of America* (1791).

The next headstone with its curved top is that of **[17] WILLIAM SMELLIE** (1740-95). Smellie was born in Edinburgh's Pleasance and trained as a printer. In his spare time

William Smellie

he attended Edinburgh University, indulging a passion for botany. So knowledgeable was he in that subject that when his Professor was absent, Smellie was employed to lecture in his place.

In 1765 he set up in business on his own as a printer and edited the first edition of the *Encyclopaedia Britannica* in the last three years of his life. To this day the stools from the print shop can be seen in the Writers' Museum in the Lawnmarket.

It was Smellie who printed the Edinburgh edition of the poems of Robert Burns and introduced him to the notorious Crochallan Fencibles (an exclusive drinking club) at Dawnay Douglas' tavern in Anchor Close next to Smellie's printing house.

Robert Burns left this portrait of William Smellie which suggests that he lived up to his last name:

Shrewd Willie Smellie to Crochallan came;
The old cock'd hat, the grey surtout, the same;
His bristling beard just rising in its might,
'Twas four long nights and days to shaving night;
His uncomb'd grizzly locks, wild staring, thatch'd;
A head for thought profound and clear, unmatch'd;
Yet tho' his caustic wit was biting-rude,
His heart was warm, benevolent and good.

Two graves further on is the pointed headstone of **[18] ALEXANDER MONRO** *Primus* (1697-1767), Professor of Anatomy for 34 years, and his son **[19] ALEXANDER**

MONRO *Secundus* (1733-1817) who held the same post for another 44 years which, added to the tenure of the post by his grandson, Monro *Tertius*, made a grand family total of 125 years!

Monro *Primus* was a brilliant anatomist who became a professor at the age of 21 and gave the Edinburgh School of Medicine its international reputation.

As a young student he was in attendance at the Battle of Prestonpans (1745), caring for the wounded. He himself died from pelvic cancer after a long and painful illness.

Monro *Secundus* was the finest physician of the Monros, with an extensive practice. Among his anatomical discoveries was the small opening in the brain now known as the 'foramen of Monro'.

Monro *Tertius*, the third member of the illustrious Monro family, is buried at the Dean Cemetery.

Facing you over the wall are the delicate silver and grey turrets of George Heriot's School, visible over the writhing black decoration of the disturbing family monument of the **[20] CHIESLIES of DALRY** built in 1679. Two noseless women on each side pray with desperate clasped hands, tiny weathered angels holding a hat over a seated scholar, while the bony figure of Death dances away from the stern finger of God emerging out of a cloud.

Buried here are the parents of John Chieslie, the man who murdered Lord President Sir George Lockhart in 1689.

The story goes that Lockhart had presided in court over a dispute between Chieslie and his wife and ordered him to pay a living allowance to her. In revenge, Chieslie, who had a violent temper, loaded his pistols on Easter Sunday 1689 and went to St Giles to lie in wait for the Lord President.

In time, Lockhart left the church and walked home to his house in what is now George IV Bridge. As he was about to enter, Chieslie shot Lockhart in the back, seriously injuring him. Chieslie was tried and sentenced to death the next day.

Tied to a wooden cart, he was dragged through the streets to the Mercat Cross, while the crowd pelted him with stones and pieces of metal. His right hand was cut off and then he was hanged in chains until his body rotted.

His relatives secretly took down the body and buried it at Dalry. From this time the Chieslie manor house at Dalry gained a reputation for strange unnatural apparitions, hauntings and the smell of fear. In the 19th century a skeleton was discovered under an old summerhouse in the garden. The right hand was missing and a pistol was tied around its neck.

Sir George Lockhart died during the siege of Edinburgh Castle in the Revolution of 1688. A cease-fire was agreed to allow his funeral to go ahead and Lockhart's body was buried inside Greyfriars Kirk (in the south-east corner).

The grave of **[21] WILLIAM CARSTARES** (1649-1715) has two grey Corinthian pillars of eroded orange-pink sandstone. Carstares was Glasgow-born, the son of a Covenanter. When his father was

Neck lock from the Old Tolbooth

forced to escape to Holland, William followed to study in Utrecht. There he met William of Orange who employed him as a spy in Britain.

Carstares was imprisoned at the Edinburgh Tolbooth in 1683 where he was tortured with the thumbscrews and the hated 'boots.' Eventually he was released and returned to Holland.

When the Revolution took place in 1688, he persuaded the new King William to introduce the Presbyterian system of Church government into Scotland. In 1703, Carstares became Principal of the University of Edinburgh.

Walk on diagonally towards the rear of the church to the triangular plot of roses between the paths. As you go, you pass the simple slabstone of **[22] NEIL GOW** Jr (1795-1823). His father, the more famous **[23] NATHANIEL GOW** (1766-1831) is also buried there.

Nathaniel was born near Dunkeld, son of the famous violinist Neil Gow Sr who taught him to play the fiddle. At the age of 16, Nathaniel became one of His Majesty's Trumpeters for Scotland and later succeeded his brother William as conductor of McGlashan's Band, which he directed for 40 years. Between 1799 and 1824 he published six highly popular collections of reels and strathspeys.

Nathaniel Gow was a favourite with George IV (then Prince of Wales) and was often asked to play for his private parties. Neil Gow Jr died before his father. He was also

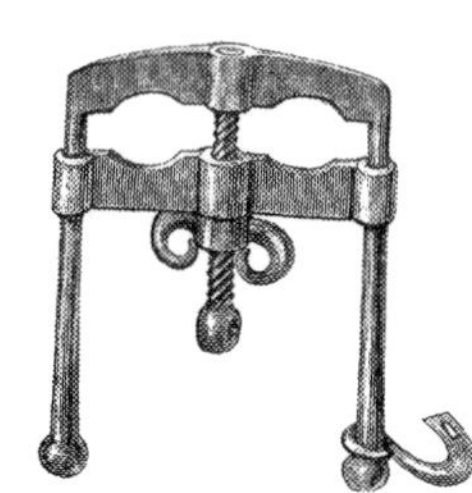
Thumbscrews

a talented composer and worked with his father as a music-seller. He composed the tune 'Bonnie Prince Charlie.'

Turn left when you reach the path and walk towards Heriot's School. As you pass, a small pink granite stone on the left of the path records that the lawyer **[24] WALTER SCOTT, WS** (1729-99) – father of the novelist Sir Walter Scott – and other members of the Scott family are buried close by. Scott himself was born near the east end of Chambers Street in Guthrie Street and later lived in George Square. His father was an elder at Greyfriars Kirk. His Episcopalian mother is buried at St John's, Princes Street.

Go past the Flodden Wall, towards the gates of Heriot's School, and then take the last path on your right. In the seventh plot on the right under a large tree is the resting-place of **[25] WILLIAM CREECH** (1745-1815), bookseller, publisher and Lord Provost. Creech took over Allan Ramsay's premises in the Luckenbooths. There all the brains of Edinburgh assembled, like bees around a honey-pot, to argue or gossip. Creech's breakfast parties were highly popular with the élite of Edinburgh.

Although Creech printed the works of the economist Adam Smith, the philosopher David Hume and the poet Robert Burns, he infuriated Burns by holding back some of the money from the sale of his poems. Burns duly took a swipe at him in print:

William Creech

A little pert, tart, tripping wight
And still his precious self his dear delight;
Who loves his own smart shadow in the streets
Better than e'er the fairest she he meets.

Return as you came, back through the arch. Turn first left. As you do so you see diagonally to the right the striking memorial pillar to **[26] GEORGE BUCHANAN** (1506-82) about 30 paces away, his bronze head sheltering inside the stone, cap on head and fur collar round his neck.

The physician Sir Robert Sibbald records that 'the skull of George Buchanan (which is more than usually spherical and so thin that the light shines through it) was de-interred from the grave and is now preserved in the library of the University of Edinburgh'.

Buchanan was Stirling-born, a relative of George Heriot. After training and teaching in Paris, Buchanan returned to Scotland as tutor to the illegitimate son of James V.

He was imprisoned by Cardinal David Beaton for writing poems criticising the Roman Catholic Church, but managed to escape while his gaolers were asleep, reaching Bordeaux in France where he later became a professor of Latin.

Another teaching post followed in Spain but he was imprisoned by the Spanish Inquisition for a year and a half. Finally, after the Reformation (1560), Buchanan was appointed Principal of St Leonard's College at the

George Buchanan

University of St Andrews and later became tutor to King James VI. One of the finest Latin poets in Europe, Buchanan was also remembered for his fierce attacks on Mary Queen of Scots and all she represented – lack of judgement in politics, Roman Catholicism and what he saw as French decadence.

Return again to the path on your left, past the large holly tree. Here we can see the full panoply of post-medieval death. The towering and magnificent tomb of **[27] ELIZABETH PATON** faces you, flanked by two semi-clothed men, framed by four Corinthian columns, the screaming head of a monster and the seated crowned figure of the Angel of Death. Below, four winged souls gaze out longingly.

Return to the path. As you do so you will notice under the tree the simple slab-stone of **[28]** Captain **JOHN PORTEOUS** (*d.*1736). Jock Porteous was the son of a Canongate tailor and trained as a tailor, but he was so difficult to handle that his father packed him off to the army where he served in Holland with the Scots Dutch Brigade.

Around 1715 Porteous returned to Edinburgh as drillmaster of the Town Guard. Three years later he was an Ensign of the Guard (which at that time consisted of 100 men in three companies) and was promoted to captain in 1726 with 30 men under his command.

Ten years later a smuggler, the dyer

Elizabeth Paton

Andrew Wilson, was sentenced to be hanged. He was taken to the Grassmarket at the foot of the West Bow where the gallows stood in a huge block of sandstone. The black-masked executioner gripped the rope, the town drummer beat out a menacing roll and Wilson was jerked up. The magistrates went for the customary 'deid-chack' (execution meal) to a nearby tavern and half an hour later waved a white rod out of the window as a signal for Wilson's body to be cut down.

As the hangman stepped forward to do this he was stoned by the crowd, one of whom cut through the rope. At the same time a hail of stones and earth was directed at the Town Guard and their captain.

Town drummer

In the confusion Porteous ordered the Guard to fire. Three civilians were killed and 12 wounded. The furious mob chased the Guard up the West Bow and in a panic the Guard fired again, killing three more.

Porteous was put on trial, found guilty, but reprieved (for political reasons) by the Regent, Queen Caroline. Immediately what were to become known as the Porteous Riots broke out. The mob stole the keys of the West Port and locked all the town gates.

Then they broke into the Guard House in the middle of the High Street, seized guns, Lochaber axes and the town drum, tried to set fire to the Tolbooth (where Porteous was being held) and managed to break in and drag him into the street where, after scorching his feet, they lynched him on a dyer's pole.

'All passion spent' reads the modern headstone – both that of Porteous and that of the mob.

Continue along the path. Take the steps down. As you reach the bottom step, look left at the small iron grill leading into a tomb under the grass. It seems to lead into an underground world, a secret city of the dead. Skull and cross-bone plaques are set into the wall. This is the last resting-place of the Spanish portrait painter **[29]** Sir **JOHN BAPTISTE DE MEDINA** (1659-1710), knighted by the Lord High Commissioner in 1707 – the last knight created in Scotland before the Act of Union (1707). Born in the Low Countries into a Spanish family, more than 40 of his portraits hang in the Royal College of Surgeons, Edinburgh, including one of Dr Archibald Pitcairne.

Further along, on the west wall is a bronze plaque to **[30] GEORGE WATSON** (1654-1723] an Edinburgh merchant who became the first accountant to the Bank of Scotland and left £12,000 to build a hospital for the maintenance and education of the male children and grandchildren of Edinburgh merchants who had fallen on hard times. The school, now known as George Watson's College, is located at Colinton Road.

Walk down over the grass along the wall of the burial ground. Here you see a sequence of highly ornate memorials, black and beige carvings filled with dramatic life – angels

John Medina

playing musical instruments, cherubs, skulls, headless figures of Justice and Mercy, twisted and deformed pillars – all full of mute noise and movement.

In front of the tomb of **[31] THOMAS BANNATYNE** (1570-1635), a wealthy merchant, a large carved slab was once imbedded in the ground. Originally this was fixed to the top of the tomb but it fell down. Now it has been magnificently restored.

On the restored slab a large fat baby sits in front of Holyrood Palace. In spite of his wealth, Bannatyne must have been a melancholy man – the observation on his tomb reads: '*What is life? A shadow, a smoke, a flower*'.

Next to the Bannatyne tomb is the grave of **[32]** Dr **JOHN HOPE** (1725-86), the son of a surgeon, educated at Edinburgh University. Hope studied botany in Paris and on his return in 1761 was made King's Botanist in Scotland and Professor of Botany and Materia Medica at the University of Edinburgh (botany being a science which, because of the use of herbs and plants in healing, was seen very much as part of the all-round training of a good doctor of medicine).

When Dr Hope was appointed there were two botanical gardens in Edinburgh: the Physic Garden beside Trinity Hospital (where the ticket office of Waverley Station is now located) and the older Royal Garden at Holyrood Palace, planted in

John Hope

1670 (and therefore the second oldest in Britain). Dr Hope united the two gardens and moved them to a site on the west side of Leith Walk, laying it out with the new Linnean system of botanical classification.

At the bottom of the wall turn right towards the two walled graves. As you approach the first you see a cylindrical stone stump jutting right out of the ground with the initials 'J. E. M.' This is the grave of **[33] JAMES DOUGLAS** (c.1516-81), the fourth Earl of Morton, and the stone is a copy of the original wooden log driven into the ground to mark burials.

Regent of Scotland (1572-78), Morton was a keen supporter of the Reformation and the alliance with England. He was dismissed for having taken part in the murder of David Rizzio, the Italian singer and secretary to Mary Queen of Scots; it was also known that he had advance warning of the plot to kill Henry Lord Darnley (Mary's husband).

Having brought over the 'Maiden' (Edinburgh's early version of the guillotine) from the Continent in 1564, it is ironic that it was that dreadful instrument that sliced off Morton's own head (much as, at a later date, Deacon William Brodie was executed with his own wooden gallows).

Morton's body was carried to the Tolbooth and secretly buried at night in Greyfriars. His head, however, was impaled on the spikes high on the roof of the Netherbow Port. Eighteen months later, by order of King James VI, the Earl of Morton's head was once again united with his body.

Walk on to the tablestone with the small

The 'Maiden'

angled stone below. **[34] Dr ARCHIBALD PITCAIRNE** (1652-1713) rests under it, a founder of the Royal College of Physicians, Professor of Physic at Leyden in Holland, a keen Jacobite, poet and wit. Although a founder member of the College of Physicians, he practised anatomy, annually dissecting a human body provided for that purpose by the Town Council. In 1701 Pitcairne also became a fellow of the Royal College of Surgeons.

He was rumoured to have been an atheist, mainly because he was sharply critical of the puritanical ways of some Kirk members and did not hide his disapproval.

While he was a distinguished physician, some of Pitcairne's published remedies seem distinctly unpalatable today:

Broth – Into a broth after skimming put a bag of linen with six red earth worms washed

Netherbow Port (demolished in 1764)

and cut in bits with shavings of hart-horn, rosemary, a date or two. Boil all a quarter of an hour longer.

Posset – Into a choppin of ale or white wine and as much water put four ounces of stoned horse-dung. Let it stand in a cold place for four hours, then pour the liquor gently out and let it stand for an hour. Boil with a sprig of rosemary and make a posset with as much milk. Sweeten it with sugar for drinking.

Pitcairne enjoyed wine and used to send his servant out after dark to bring more bottles into his cellar. He was reputed to have been 'drunk twice every day'.

An ardent, but secret, Jacobite, Pitcairne asked for several bottles of wine to be buried in his grave with the proviso that they were to be drunk only when a Stuart came once more to the throne of Scotland. However, some decades later when his gravestone was being restored, the bottles had mysteriously disappeared!

Walk on four paces – at your feet lies **[35] JAMES CRAIG** (1744-95), who at 23 years of age won the competition to design Edinburgh's New Town.

Craig (whose instruments and plans can still be seen in the Museum of Edinburgh in the Canongate) also designed the once-fashionable Merchant Street under George IV Bridge, the Gothic Observatory on Calton Hill built for the astronomer Thomas Short and the entrance to Leith Fort.

The quotation on Craig's stone is from his uncle, the poet James Thomson's 'Prospect of Great Britain':

August, around, what public works I see!
Lo! Stately streets, lo! Squares that court the breeze,
Even fram'd with elegance the plain retreat,
The private dwelling. Certain in his aim,
Taste, never idly working, saves expence.

Now turn half right towards the large obelisk eight paces away under the trees. Far off, from the Highlands, you can almost hear the bagpipes calling on the wind. The monument is decorated with a basket-hilted claymore, a targe (shield), shepherd's crook, hunting-horn, scrolls of poems, a rifle, a partridge, an antlered deer, a rabbit and a pistol. This monument commemorates the great Highland poet and soldier **[36] DUNCAN BAN MACINTYRE** (1724-1812) known as 'Fair Duncan of the Songs'.

Duncan ban Macintyre

Macintyre was a soldier with the Breadalbane Fencibles who fought against the Jacobites at the Battle of Falkirk Muir in 1746. Shortly afterwards the Fencibles were disbanded and Macintyre worked as a forester and gamekeeper for 20 years until unfairly dismissed. He had no choice but to leave his family and glen. To get his revenge he wrote a satirical poem on the subject. Reaching the city of Edinburgh, he joined the Town Guard.

With his wife he distilled and sold illicit whisky in a Lawnmarket 'howff'. Although he never learned to read, memorising his poems instead, he became one of the major Gaelic poets and travelled throughout the Highlands, wearing Highland dress, selling his works. On his head he wore a checked bonnet from which hung the large bushy tail of a wild animal. A badger's skin was fastened by a belt in front of him, a sword was at his side and a soldier's wallet strapped across his broad shoulders. To this day a Gaelic-speaking service is held regularly at Greyfriars Kirk.

Next, walk east towards the green hedge. Go round the side of the hedge to the left, to the tall monument at the wall above Candlemaker Row – the **[37] MARTYRS MONUMENT** with its triangular pediment on top, Ionic columns and large scrolls on each side framing the text of a long prayer to those who died for the Covenant.

Greyfriars Kirk has an important place in the history of the National Covenant. The Covenant was a protest by Scottish Presbyterians against the new English forms of worship introduced by Charles I. The first copy of the document was drawn up in the Tailors' Hall in the Cowgate and then brought to Greyfriars on 28 February 1638 to be signed by nobles and lairds, before being taken back to the Cowgate again to be signed by ministers and representatives of the towns.

In June 1679 at Bothwell Bridge the Covenanters were finally defeated. Twelve hundred of them were roped in pairs and taken to Edinburgh where they were held at

Greyfriars churchyard (then a grass park of some three acres surrounded by high walls), the wounded being cared for in Heriot's Hospital close by. Here for five months the Covenanters lived in the open with no shelter and little food.

Within two weeks 400 of them were sentenced to be transported to the Plantations in the West Indies but many were also released after promising not to rebel again. In early August one Covenanter, John Kid, was tortured by the 'boots' which crushed his legs. He and another Covenanter were then publicly executed. By November, only 340 prisoners were left. Five were hanged in chains and 250 sent by sea to the West Indies. Off Orkney the ship sank in a storm – most were drowned, trapped below the decks.

The Martyrs Monument (a copy – the original stone can be seen in the Museum of Edinburgh in the Canongate) records that:

> From May 27th 1661, when the most noble Marquis of Argyle was beheaded, to the 17th of February 1688 when Mr Renwick suffered, were one way or other Murdered and Destroyed for the same Cause, about 18,000, of whom were executed at Edinburgh almost a hundred of Noblemen,

> Gentlemen, Ministers and Others, noble Martyrs for Jesus Christ. The most of them lie here.

To the west of the monument, in a long trench, more than 100 Covenanters were buried. Under the inscription a bed of flowers grows throughout most of the year.

Turn back towards the church and walk to the middle of the retaining wall, below the large expanse of grass bordering the church. Above the terrace, in an unmarked grave, lies **[38] WILLIAM RITCHIE** (1781-1831), solicitor and, with his friend Charles Maclaren, founder of *The Scotsman* newspaper (1817).

In the middle of the terrace wall, a large urn (almost an Aladdin's lamp) stands below an inscription dedicated to **[39] HENRY MACKENZIE** (1745-1831), an Edinburgh solicitor who became Attorney for the Crown in Scotland. He was best known as a writer of essays, plays and novels and widely referred to as *The Man of Feeling* from the title of his popular novel of that name published in 1771, a book which wallowed in excessive 'tear-jerking'.

Turn left and walk over to the cobbled path. Then go right at the black street-lamp. When you reach the cherry trees, go left across the grass towards Candlemaker Row.

Surrounded by pink gravel and pink cobbles is the pink and grey stone of **[40] JOHN GRAY** (1813-58), standing close beside the old tablestone under which his dog Bobby sheltered for many years.

John Gray – 'Auld Jock' – a police

constable, lived in the Cowgate with his trained police dog, Bobby. PC Gray saw to the safety of the livestock at the weekly market in the Grassmarket. In 1857 he contracted tuberculosis and died the following year. His faithful Skye terrier, **[41] 'GREYFRIARS BOBBY'**, accompanied the funeral procession and stayed at his master's graveside for 14 years.

As you leave the churchyard, stop beside the pink granite headstone at the entrance erected to Bobby by the Dog Aid Society in 1981.

Just outside the entrance to Greyfriars Kirk once stood John Traill's Refreshment Rooms where Bobby was fed for his 14 long years of watching and waiting.

In 1867, Bobby (legally a stray dog and liable to be put down) was licensed by Edinburgh's Lord Provost in recognition of his extraordinary faithfulness. His statue by the sculptor William Brodie, was later erected by Baroness Burdett-Coutts opposite the churchyard entrance, a drinking-fountain below it to quench the thirst of weary passers-by.

Greyfriars Bobby's dish, collar and the cup from the drinking-fountain (shut off in 1957) are in the Museum of Edinburgh.

Now find somewhere to sit in the churchyard, breathe deeply and close your eyes for a moment. Focus your thoughts on a number of other great names buried here in unmarked graves – like the unfortunate **[42]** Bailie **JOHN MACMORRAN** (1553-95) who was shot and killed trying to end a

Greyfriars Bobby

sit-in by the boys of the High School in 1595 when they protested over a reduction in their autumn holiday.

When the culprit was found it turned out he was William Sinclair, son of the Chancellor of Caithness. The boy's wealthy relatives used their influence with King James VI and Sinclair was given a free pardon – a decision which was extremely unpopular in Edinburgh. Macmorran is buried on the east side of the church, the exact location unknown.

Among other figures drifting towards you in the haze are **[43] GEORGE JAMESONE** (1588-1644), one of the first Scottish portrait-painters, the 'Van Dyck of Scotland' who trained with Rubens in Antwerp; and the brilliant **[44] JAMES GREGORY** (1638-75) who first suggested a practical design for a reflecting telescope. Neither grave is marked.

Keeper of the Advocates Library for almost 50 years, **[45] THOMAS RUDDIMAN** (1674-1757), is only remembered in an elegant plaque inside the church. In collaboration with the printer and publisher Robert Fairbairn, Ruddiman brought out the works of the poets Gavin Douglas, William Drummond of Hawthornden, George Buchanan and Allan Ramsay.

Now coming into focus is **[46] WILLIAM GED** (1690-1749), a goldsmith who invented stereotyping which made it possible to take a metal cast of a whole page of type and so speed up the printing process. His grave is on the east wall, north of the graveyard entrance.

Two great comedians stroll into sight – **[47] JOHN KAY** (1742-1826), barber and prince of caricaturists (whose 'Edinburgh Portraits' sent up Edinburgh society as only a hair-dresser could) is buried near the north end of the old west wall.

Striding towards you now is the inimitable **[48] WILLIAM McGONAGALL** (1825-1902), prince of clowns, the 'world's worst poet', who was born and who died in the Cowgate.

In November 1895 he performed his poem 'The Battle of Bannockburn' to the fun-loving Junior Section of the Leith Liberal Club, waving his stick wildly as he proclaimed, *'The Englishmen from the Scots did fly, And left many thousands on the field quite dead to die . . . '* In his heyday as a travelling tragedian McGonagall used to play Shakespeare's *Macbeth* but when he was stabbed to death on stage he would refuse to 'die'. McGonagall is buried in an unmarked pauper's grave to the north of the church.

Have a quiet giggle at his amiable nonsense and then slowly open your eyes.

John Kay

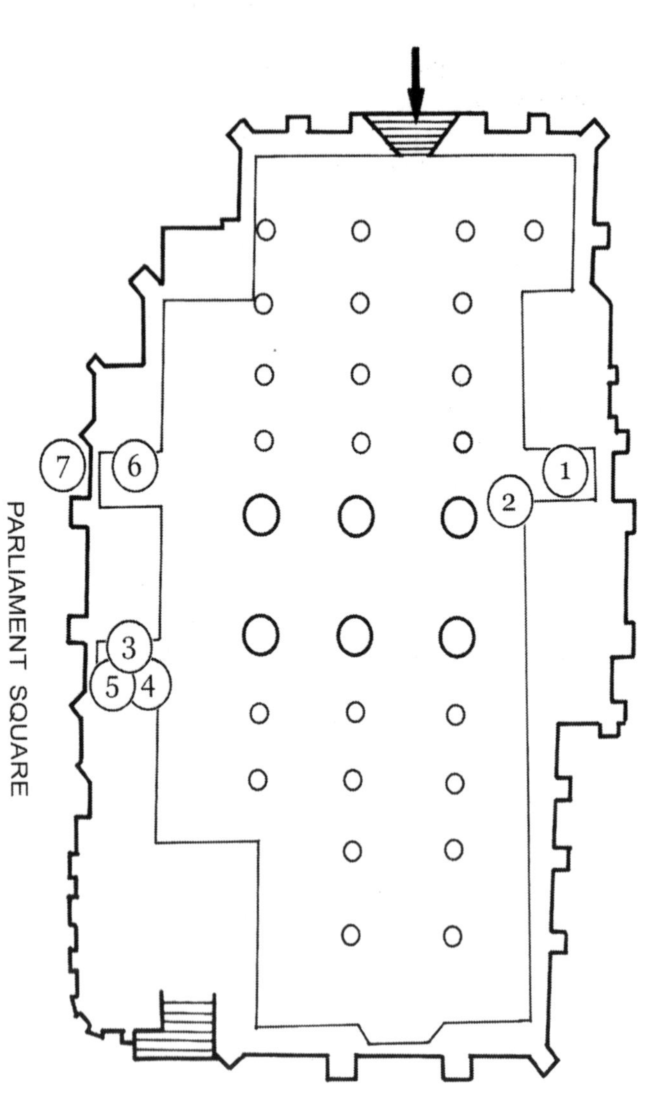

St Giles Cathedral

Location – High Street

St Giles

The earliest church building on the site of the present St Giles probably dates from around the year 1140.

Traditionally, St Giles was the burial-place chosen by the rich and famous (who would be buried *inside* the church); the rest of the parishioners would be buried in the churchyard of St Giles (which stretched down the south slope of the High Street as far as the Cowgate). St Giles was the main burial place for all the people of the burgh until 1566 when over crowding forced it to close.

In 1581 the Reformed Church in Scotland prohibited burials inside church buildings; however, some burials still took place inside St Giles as late as 1765.

St Giles, 1878

The inside of the church has seen many changes: in about 1581 stone walls divided the interior into three separate congregations. These partitions were removed in 1633 but were rebuilt in 1639, not being finally removed till 1882.

During these extensive 'improvements' made between 1829 and 1833 many of the pre- and post-Reformation tombs were destroyed. The result is that most of the memorials to be seen in St Giles today dedicated to persons who died before 1879 (when Lord Provost William Chambers proposed the restoration of the interior into a single church) are Victorian: Regent Moray (1864), the Earl of Montrose (1888) and the Earl of Argyll (1894). The many interior monuments were erected as part of Chambers' efforts to have St Giles recognised as the Westminster Abbey of Scotland.

Enter through the main western door under the intricate patterns of stone binding on stone. On the wind you may hear the distant and contradictory voices which once worshipped in the ancient kirk.

Turn left into the church. Inside all is still and dark – a place of peace now. Pass the garlanded kneeling angel, even though she gracefully offers you a white marble scallop shell.

Up in the mysterious shadows of the roof, stone locks on to rugged stone. The second chapel you come to on the left, past the dark bronze figure of John Knox, holds the tomb of cross-eyed **[1]** Archibald Campbell (*Gillespie Gruatnach*), the **MARQUESS of ARGYLL** (1607-61), clutching a sword with a basket-hilt, his head on a cushion, his right hand on the Bible (with a sprig of heather beside it), his feet crossed in elegant shoes.

Argyll was a devout Presbyterian, controlling his enormous estates from Inverary Castle. As chief of the Clan Campbell, he had 5,000 men at his disposal. When Charles I came to Scotland in 1641 to make peace with the Covenanters, he created Campbell, their leader, the first Marquess of Argyll.

Seven years later the most fervent Covenanters marched on Edinburgh, swept the Government aside and left Argyll in almost complete control – he was thus able to allow Oliver Cromwell into Edinburgh with a warm welcome from the citizens.

After Charles I's execution, the captured Earl of Montrose was imprisoned in Edinburgh, tortured and taken up the High Street under the scornful eyes of Argyll himself, who watched from Moray House.

Marquess of Argyll

The Old Tolbooth

Montrose was hanged at the Mercat Cross on 21 May 1650; his limbs hacked off and his head stuck on the Tolbooth roof as a grisly warning.

In 1651 it was Argyll who placed the crown on Charles II at Scone. But his luck was about to turn – only ten years after Montrose's dismembered body was given a hero's burial at Holyrood, Argyll was taken as a prisoner to Edinburgh Castle, and after he was executed in the High Street, his head was also impaled on the Tolbooth.

As you leave the tomb, look at the first pillar on your left. There, a brass inscription framed in red polished marble commemorates **[2]** James Dalrymple, **VISCOUNT STAIR** (1619-95), Professor of Philosophy by the age of 23. He gave up academic life and became an advocate in 1648. He was made a judge by Oliver Cromwell in 1657 and, at the Restoration, this appointment was confirmed by Charles II.

Crown of Scotland

He became Lord President of the Court of Session in 1670 and two years later was elected MP for Wigtown.

Having fought for the Covenanters as a young man, Lord Stair did not approve of the harsh treatment which the Covenanters were later given. His wife was taken into custody for attending Covenanter meetings and Lord Stair was accused of complicity.

He escaped to Holland in 1682 but was charged with treason for being involved in the 1679 Rebellion and the Rye House Plot. In 1688, however, he returned with William of Orange and was reinstated as Lord President.

Stair was best known for his monumental work, *The Institutions of the Law of Scotland* (1681), which laid down the basis of legal practice in Scotland, regularising it into a coherent system.

The mysterious disappearance of his daughter Janet in 1669, only a month after her wedding, inspired Sir Walter Scott's novel *The Bride of the Lammermuir*, and Donizetti's opera *Lucia di Lammermoor*.

Cross to the opposite side of the church in the direction of Parliament House (south).

On the left-hand side of the mighty organ is the Chepman Aisle, the resting-place of **[3] WALTER CHEPMAN** (*c.*1473-*c.*1538), an Edinburgh merchant and clerk in the office of the King's Secretary (1494). He financed the first Scottish commercial printing press under the direction of the master printer Andrew Myllar.

Seal of St Giles

Myllar had trained as a printer at Rouen in France where he had two books published. He set up as a bookseller in Edinburgh, and in 1507 he and Chepman were given the Royal Patent to set up a printing press with all the tools and equipment necessary and the craftsmen to operate it.

Myllar's craftsmen and the Gothic typefaces were French. It is this which makes the earliest Scottish printed books different from those printed in England by William Caxton (who was trained in Germany). The press of Chepman and Myllar in the Cowgate was in production between 1508 and 1510. All that remains today of their printed books are some poetic tales, parts of the poem 'The Wallace' and the *Aberdeen Breviary* (clerical prayerbook).

In 1513 Chepman used his wealth to found a chapel dedicated to the memory of his patron James IV of Scotland and was himself buried there, facing the Marquess of Montrose, with an inscription by that other great publisher and conservationist, Lord Provost William Chambers.

Opposite Chepman is the tomb of **[4]** John Graham, 3rd **EARL of MONTROSE** (1547-1608) who fought at the Battle of Langside on Regent Moray's side. James VI thought highly of him and in 1584 he was appointed a Lord of Session (judge). He had been chancellor of the jury at the trial of Regent Morton in 1581.

When James VI became King James I of England (and moved to London), Montrose was made Viceroy of Scotland.

In the same tomb is his grandson James

Graham, **[5]** 1st **MARQUESS of MONTROSE** (1612-50), a true romantic man of action. Now you see him lying on his tomb, with a fresh bunch of white heather bound with tartan ribbon or a blood-red rose. Beside him is a copy of the National Covenant – he was one of the first to sign – which inspired him to perform incredible feats of soldiering under the skilled guidance of *Colkitto* (Alastair MacDonald).

Montrose worked hard to persuade King Charles I to accept the National Covenant. Then Montrose changed sides, opposing the Covenanters. Charles made him Lieutenant-General in Scotland and Montrose began a series of masterly victories. At Tippermuir (also known as Tibbermore) he defeated the Covenanters, captured Aberdeen and started off on unpredictable marches through the Highlands. He surprised the Marquess of Argyll in his own castle of Inverary and then again at Inverlochy in the middle of winter.

After going into exile on the Continent, Montrose returned to Scotland in 1650, marching down from Orkney. However, on this occasion he was finally defeated and taken prisoner.

When Montrose arrived in Edinburgh he had already been declared a traitor. He was met by the town officials, his hands were tied and he was fastened to a seat in the executioner's wagon. In this degrading posture he was taken up the Royal Mile, past Moray House

James Graham, Marquess of Montrose

(where the Marquess of Argyll left a wedding reception to watch Montrose as he passed by).

In his cell Montrose composed his own blistering epitaph:

Let them bestow on ev'ry Airth a Limb;
Open all my Veins, that I may swim
To Thee my Saviour, in that Crimson Lake;
Then place my purboiled Head upon a Stake;
Scatter my Ashes, throw them in the Air:
Lord (since Thou know'st where all these Atoms are)
I'm hopeful, once Thou'lt recollect my Dust,
And confident Thou'lt raise me with the Just.

He proved to be an accurate prophet of his own fate. However, in 1661 the many parts of his dismembered body were reunited and buried with due pomp and ceremony.

Go past the organ. In the next aisle is the austere grey monument to **[6]** the **EARL of MORAY** (1531-70), James Stewart, illegitimate son of James V (and the half brother of Mary Queen of Scots).

He was a statesman with a broad vision and deep understanding of political events. Although he supported the Reformers, believing them to be the best hope for Scotland's future, he also allowed Queen Mary to worship with the Catholic liturgy in her private chapel. But he saw to it that the future James VI received a Protestant education and understood the ways of the English, so that when the time came he could be king of both Scotland and England.

Moray was a key figure in the government of Scotland up to the point in

Bothwell and Mary

1565 when Mary decided to marry Darnley. Moray then supported Darnley's resentment of the growing power of Mary's well-bred Italian secretary, the suave David Riccio with the dark, seductive bass singing voice.

Later, when Mary married Bothwell, the Earl of Moray was safe in England giving evidence against his half-sister. And after the Queen abdicated, he became Regent for the young King James.

In January 1570 Regent Moray was travelling from Stirling to Edinburgh when he was shot dead by Hamilton of Bothwellhaugh (whose life, ironically, he had saved at the Battle of Langside two years before).

John Knox preached at Moray's funeral and an inscription by the poet George Buchanan was fixed into the monument. In 1829 the monument was destroyed during the alterations to the church. The original brass plate was later set in a new monument presented by the 12th Earl of Moray in 1864.

Leave the church the way you came. In Parliament Square, turn left and make for the lead statue of Charles II on horseback.

Now you may hear a powerful voice echoing round the porticoes of the High Court. For, not far below the statue of the Merry Monarch, in parking lot No 44, is the grave of **[7] JOHN KNOX** (1512-72).

Knox, buried in St Giles churchyard some years after it was declared closed, was the leader of the Reformation in Scotland. Trained as a Catholic priest and papal notary (solicitor), he was an expert in canon law. His skill in public speaking was sharpened by his legal training and his subsequent bitter experiences of life as a French galley-slave.

Knox was born near Haddington, East Lothian. The executions of Scottish Reformers such as Patrick Hamilton (1528) and George Wishart (1546) hardened his conviction that the Church in Scotland badly needed to be reformed. To help him in this mammoth task, he turned first to England for support.

John Knox's House, early twentieth century

John Knox's pulpit, St Giles

Following the assassination of Cardinal David Beaton at St Andrews in 1546, Knox then returned to Scotland to work for the Reformed community as a Protestant minister. However, St Andrews was captured by the French and Knox was made a galley-slave for two years until King Edward VI of England secured his release.

In England, Knox was a minister at Newcastle, Berwick and in London before being appointed Royal Chaplain. He advised Archbishop Cranmer on the drawing up of the new Articles of Religion, contributed to the writing of the *Second Prayer Book* and later composed his own *History of the Reformation in Scotland* (1587).

During the reign of the Catholic Queen Mary, Knox was in Frankfurt and Geneva, absorbing the Reformed theology of John Calvin. He returned once more to Scotland in 1559, becoming minister of St Giles. In his *Book of Discipline* (1560 and 1568) he set out a far-reaching plan for a Church with no bishops, a programme of universal comprehensive education and a nationwide system of poor relief.

Knox, with a hypnotic gift for denunciation and prophetic criticism, was a powerful opponent of the French attitudes of Mary Queen of Scots. In 1572 he preached in St Giles for the last time, being so weak he had to be supported in the arms of his friends.

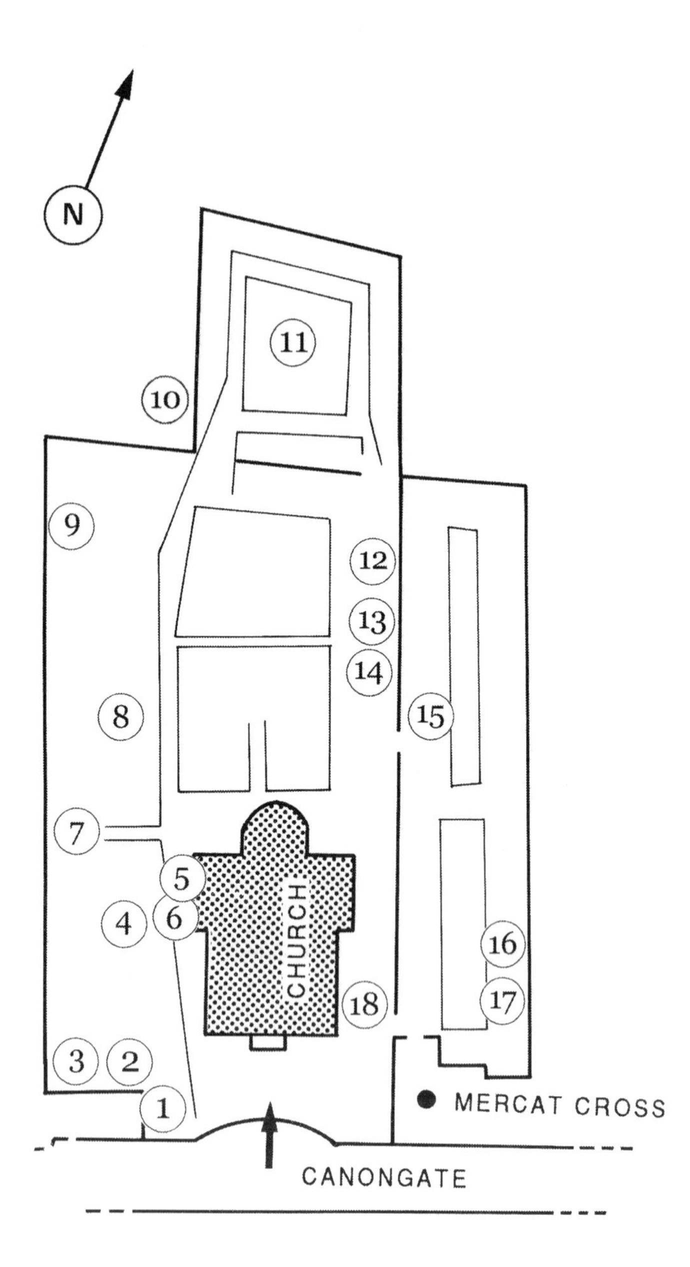

Canongate Churchyard

Location – Canongate

CANONGATE

The first thing that strikes you about the Canongate Kirk is the weathered skull and antlers of a deer high on the roof above the pillared porch. This commemorates the legendary escape of King David I from a wild stag in the nearby Forest of Drumsheugh and his dazzling vision of the Cross between its antlers. It is the traditional symbol of the Canongate.

For centuries Holyrood Abbey was the parish church for the Canongate but in 1686 King James VII turned the Abbey church into a Roman Catholic Chapel Royal for the Order of the Thistle and made the parishioners go elsewhere. In 1691 the Canongate Kirk was opened as a replacement.

Go through the main gate under a canopy of ornamental cherry trees and turn first left. Set into the wall of the Canongate Tolbooth which faces you, overlooking a small plot of

Canongate Kirk

George Drummond

lush grass framed by railings, is the simple stone commemorating [1] Lord Provost **GEORGE DRUMMOND** (1687-1766) whose true monument is Edinburgh's New Town.

As a tall Perthshire lad, Drummond had a clear head for figures. By the age of 20 he had become Accountant General of Excise. He rose rapidly through the ranks of Edinburgh Town Council, took part in the General Assembly of the Church of Scotland and played an influential role in the appointment of many of the finest professors at Edinburgh University (which was controlled by the Town Council).

As a soldier, he fought for the Hanoverians at the battle of Sherrifmuir in 1715. When the Jacobites attacked Edinburgh 30 years later he commanded the 1st (College) Company. Unfortunately, his men turned out to be too timid to fight and ran away!

Drummond was Edinburgh's greatest Lord Provost (he served six terms from 1725 to 1764), the driving force behind the building of the New Town, and a founder of the Royal Infirmary in 1738, as well as the North Bridge in 1763. He also backed the construction of the City Chambers (then known as the Royal Exchange), the elegant St Cecilia's concert hall in the Cowgate and the draining of the Nor' Loch to form Princes Street Gardens.

Drummond was a staunch Whig in politics and a man with deep Presbyterian religious convictions. He married four times and had 14 children. His diary, written in 1738, shows him continually dogged by debt and self-doubt – 'I am now entered my fifty-second year and alas how little progress have I made on my way to heaven'.

Go left again to the rear of the Tolbooth to the burial-ground of the economist **[2] ADAM SMITH** (1723-90), framed by high black railings topped by graceful *fleurs-de-lys*.

The handsome but austere monument set against the wall is topped by an urn; a bearded classical head stares from the centre of an arch of radiating rays of light and a small medallion hangs from a ribbon with simple swathes of cloth falling away at each side (it is almost exactly the same design as the gravestone of Joseph Black in Greyfriars).

Smith, born in Kirkcaldy in Fife, is best known as a pioneer of Economics. His *Wealth of Nations* (1776) had an immediate impact on politicians and a lasting influence on businessmen.

Smith showed how the division of labour could improve productivity and also how value comes from the labour used in production. He taught that in a market

Adam Smith

economy the profit motive could be made to work for the good of the whole community.

He was educated at the universities of Glasgow and Oxford, lecturing first in English Literature at Edinburgh, then becoming Professor of Moral Philosophy at Glasgow. In later years he tutored the Duke of Buccleuch, receiving a pension for life. With the Duke he visited Paris where he met the philosophers David Hume and Voltaire.

He ended his days as a Commissioner for Customs and then settled into a comfortable lifestyle at nearby Panmure House in the Canongate where he enjoyed entertaining his friends right up to his death.

One of Smith's most likeable characteristics was his continual absent-mindedness – this led him into some hilarious situations. While Professor of Moral Philosophy in Glasgow Smith took a friend to see a well-known leather tannery. The two of them were standing on a plank laid over the tanning-pit, Dr Smith talking excitedly about his favourite topic – the division of labour. He completely forgot where he was, stepped to one side and fell head first into the dye-bath. He was pulled out straight away, stripped, wrapped in blankets and carried home in a sedan chair where he complained that he was about to die from the cold!

On another occasion he was visited one morning at his home in Edinburgh – Panmure House. Deep in conversation again, Smith took a piece of bread and butter, rolled the two together for some time in his fingers and dropped it into the open teapot. When he came to drink the tea he complained that it was the worst he had ever tasted.

While working as a Commissioner for Customs in the Royal Exchange (now the Edinburgh City Chambers), Smith approached the entrance and was met by the guard, a tall impressive man dressed in a large red cloak decorated with lace and holding a stout seven foot high pole of office.

As each Commissioner entered, the guard would go through an elaborate routine of saluting with his pole. When Smith approached, the guard presented his staff like a soldier presenting a rifle.

As if in a trance, Smith started to imitate the guard by presenting his bamboo walking-cane, holding it in the middle with both hands, carrying out this operation with complete seriousness.

The annoyed guard lowered the pole and stepped back to let the Commissioner pass. Instead of walking past, Smith stopped opposite the guard and lowered his cane to the same angle.

Puzzled, the guard went up the stairs, his pole raised in front of him. The author of *The Wealth of Nations* followed with his bamboo cane held in precisely the same way, imitating exactly each step taken by the guard.

At the door of the hall the guard again stepped back, saluted with his pole and bowed with great dignity. Smith repeated his every movement, bowing back to him. When he got into the room and was told what he had done, Smith could remember nothing about the incident.

A town guard

Next to the grave of Adam Smith is the grey granite sarcophagus of the Aberdonian **[3] JAMES GREGORY** (1753-1821) and other members of his family. Gregory's lasting claim to fame is not so much his professorship of Medicine at Edinburgh or being the leading consultant in Scotland, but in his marvellous brown 'Gregory's Mixture' made from magnesia, rhubarb and ginger – which brought relief to upset stomachs for many generations. He was also a strong believer in blood-letting, purging, cold baths and tartar emetics.

Gregory was an outspoken, energetic man with a sharp sense of humour. He had a quick temper and on one occasion raised his stick on a fellow doctor, Professor James Hamilton, and hit him severely about the body. He was fined £100 but asserted that he was ready to pay double for another chance to hit the Professor!

Now turn towards the classical facade of the former Royal High School far above you on the slopes of Calton Hill. Walk towards the far end of the church where you see the single round window. Just before you get there look to your left at the tall Greek obelisk to the philanthropic plumber **[4] GEORGE CHALMERS** (1773-1836) who left £30,000 at his death for the construction of Chalmers Hospital in Lauriston Place. The elegance of his monument matches his generosity.

James Gregory

The Runciman brothers

From the Chalmers obelisk walk directly to the church. Under the round window is the memorial to two artist brothers, each facing the other – **[5] ALEXANDER RUNCIMAN** (1736-85) bare-headed; and **[6] JOHN RUNCIMAN** (1744-68) with a natty hat, coat and fancy lace at his neck.

Having studied the works of Raphael and Michelangelo in Italy, Alexander executed a number of mural paintings in Scotland. One of these can be seen (partially exposed) on the ceiling of the nearby St Patrick's Church in the Cowgate. Alexander was a sociable but fiery-tempered man. He eventually dropped dead in West Nicolson Street, partly as a result of the physical stress of lying on his back while painting ceilings. His brother John was a promising painter but died tragically young while on a visit to Naples.

Continue down the path in the direction of Calton Hill. As you reach the end of the church turn hard left up a path of pink granite chips. Walk 11 paces to the simple vertical grey slabstone with its plot of roses fenced off by heavy chain-links. This is the grave of the young poet **[7] ROBERT FERGUSSON** (1750-74), who died in tragic circumstances and whose alert bronze likeness now welcomes visitors quizzically to the church from the Canongate pavement.

In spite of his St Andrews degree, Fergusson toiled as a humble legal clerk, writing songs which he performed at private houses across Edinburgh. His end was tragic – sudden changes of mood and a hint of mental instability produced by a serious fall down a flight of steps, led to him being committed to the Bedlam (asylum for the insane). There he tragically took his own life and was buried in a pauper's grave.

Fergusson, whom Robert Burns greatly admired, wrote with a fresh and colourful eye, full of humour and observation. Two of his best poems are 'Caller Oysters' and 'Auld Reekie', the latter a celebration of the sights and sounds of street life in the capital:

Now Morn, with bonny purple smiles,
Kisses the air-cock o' Saunt Giles;
Rakin their een, the servant lasses
Early begin their lies and clashes.
On stair, wi' tub or pat in hand,
The barefoot housemaids loe to stand,
That antrin folk may ken how snell
Auld Reekie will at mornin smell.

Statue of Robert Fergusson

While in the Bedlam he suffered from delusions, imagining himself a king, putting a crown of pleated straw on his head. After two months, he died in his cell on his bed of straw, in the terrors of the night, amid the howls of insanity. There was no one to help or pity him.

When Robert Burns came to Edinburgh in 1787 he was so angry at the absence of a memorial to Fergusson that he asked permission from the Town Council to pay for a stone and epitaph. Burns' words on the stone read:

No sculptured marble here, nor pompous lay,
No storied Urn, nor animated Bust;
This simple Stone directs Pale Scotia's way
To pour her Sorrows o'er her poet's Dust.

Robert Louis Stevenson had also planned to add some words of his own at Fergusson's grave but he died before he could do so.

Now walk down over the grass towards Nelson's Monument on the Calton Hill high above. At about 26 paces is the slabstone dedicated in 1766 to the **[8] SOCIETY OF COACH-DRIVERS**, whose members were buried anonymously around the stone. On the top is a skull gnawing a thigh-bone – a reminder that Death is never far away (especially on the roads!) Below, a coach and four rattles over the North Bridge (built only three years previously), the coach-driver cracking his whip.

Walk diagonally downwards towards the end of the boundary wall on your left. The third last memorial on the wall (head-high below three coping-stones), is of the Revd

Fergusson's Grave

Alexander Brunton and his wife, the novelist **[9] MARY BRUNTON** (1778-1818).

Mary was born in Orkney. She was a good musician and spoke French and Italian. At the age of 19 she eloped with a young minister. Much of her adult life was spent as a country minister's wife in East Lothian but when her husband moved to Edinburgh as minister of Greyfriars Kirk she wrote her first novel, *Self-Control* (1811), enlivened with exciting adventures which thinly disguised a strong moral message. Then she wrote a second, *Discipline* (1815). Her husband became Professor of Oriental Languages and Moderator of the General Assembly of the Church of Scotland. She had begun a third novel when she died giving birth to her first baby (still-born).

Turn right and go to the path, walking towards the slim white Gothic steeple

Dugald Stewart's monument
with Edinburgh Castle in the background

monument. At the path turn left down to the great mass of ivy covering the black and beige stones of the tomb built for **[10] DUGALD STEWART** (1753-1828), Professor of Moral Philosophy.

Stewart was a magnetic lecturer with a national reputation. Many students lodged at his Canongate home, one of them being a future Prime Minister, Lord Palmerston. In his early days as a lecturer he would get up at 3am and prepare his lectures while walking in the garden.

Lord Cockburn records that 'he was the finest reader I have ever heard. To me his lectures were as the opening of the heavens'.

Now look up. On the brow of Calton Hill, high above Dugald Stewart's tomb, is the Greek temple designed in his honour by W H Playfair and erected in 1832.

Look back to the Canongate churchyard. Standing alone in the centre of the grassy enclosure is a very tall (26 foot) red granite pillar decorated at the bottom by crossed muskets with fixed bayonets and a soldier's ammunition belt. It was erected by the proprietor of the nearby Holyrood Glassworks, William Ford in May 1880.

This commemorates the many **[11] SOLDIERS** who died while on garrison duty at Edinburgh Castle between 1692 and 1880 and who are buried around the pillar, the Castle being part of the Canongate parish. The monument was erected in the presence of men of the 71st Regiment, then quartered at the Castle, the Chaplain to the Forces in Scotland and a number of Holyrood High Constables. It bears the inscription:

Johann Frederick Lampe

Their country's sons will around this stone
Oft speak of the deeds of the brave,
And gratefully look on the grassy sod
That grows o'er the soldiers' grave.

If you close your eyes you can hear the sounds of battle, the trumpets, the skirl of the bagpipes, the thunder of cannon and the desperate screams of dying men.

Now turn back to the church along the other boundary through the doorway in the wall. Faintly you hear a very different sound – the jovial tones of an 18th century bassoon running up and down the scale and the tuning up of a theatre orchestra.

Continue up the path towards the largest enclosed grave on your left. Three graves before you reach it is the badly eroded but honey-coloured memorial wall sculpture to **[12] JOHANN FREDERICK LAMPE** (1703-51), a German musician and composer, reputed to have been Handel's favourite bassoon-player in London. Lampe is believed to have played the contra-bassoon at the coronation of George I. The almost illegible epitaph on his monument announces that Lampe 'was summoned to join the heavenly concert with the blessed Choir above'.

In 1750 Lampe arrived in Edinburgh as musical director for the Canongate Theatre in Old Playhouse Close conducting, among other operas, Handel's *Acis* and *Galatea* (with Lampe's wife singing) – this being the only recorded performance of a major Handel work given in Edinburgh during Handel's lifetime. At the Edinburgh pleasure-gardens Lampe also introduced the London style of open-air concerts – a fashion which still continues today in Princes Street Gardens.

He composed around 13 operas and three pantomimes and wrote a book on musical theory – *A plain and compendious method of Teaching Thorough-Bass* (1737). An extract from this work can be seen carved at the top of his monument, the pages held open by two winged cherubs.

Lampe also composed tunes for the Methodist hymn-writer Charles Wesley (who came to Edinburgh on numerous occasions)

William Fettes

and Wesley in turn wrote two hymns for Lampe.

Perhaps you can smell a whiff of tea and coffee brewing on the hob? Proceed to the imposing mausoleum of **[13]** Sir **WILLIAM FETTES** (1750-1836), tea and wine merchant, Lord Provost and founder of Fettes College on his estate of Comely Bank.

Look down at the small brass plaque on the left front of the monument. It records the burial nearby of **[14] JAMES BALLANTYNE** (1772-1833), a Kelso solicitor turned printer and publisher who printed Sir Walter Scott's *The Minstrelsy of the Scottish Border* as well as his novels. Ballantyne lived at St John Street in the Canongate and his printing business was just below the Calton Hill. He was a generous, sociable character. In fact, on the day of Ballantyne's funeral, standing at the graveside of his friend, Scott whispered, 'I feel as if there would be less sunshine for me from this day forth.'

Walk on again up the slope and turn first left between two gate-pillars into the other

Fettes College

section of the churchyard. Immediately on your left is the stately monument marked 'Earnock and Dalnair' with the bronze profile of the landscape painter **[15] HUGH** 'Greek' **WILLIAMS** (1773-1829) set into the pink granite.

Williams was born on his father's ship during a voyage to the West Indies. He was orphaned early and brought up in Edinburgh by a grandmother who had married a cultured Italian. He encouraged Williams to draw and paint. Success in painting Highland landscapes was followed by a tour to Italy and Greece. This led to an outpouring of water-colours. Lord Cockburn wrote that he was 'by far the finest painter in water-colours that Scotland has yet produced'.

He married a Miss Millar of Earnock and not many years later died from an incurable disease which he had endured with heroic cheerfulness.

Walk forward to the boundary-wall and turn right. Now you hear a new kind of music – a plaintive Scots song sung by an Ayrshire lad. The third plot on the left is the burial-ground of **[16] WILLIAM**, Lord **CRAIG** (1745-1813), Senator of the College of Justice and his cousin **[17]** Mrs **AGNES MACLEHOSE** (Nancy Craig) (1759-1841). Her delightful profile can be seen on a golden plaque just as it might have charmed her friend Robert Burns (a relationship of which Lord Craig disapproved). She wears a low-cut gown, a scarf twisted through her hair.

Nancy Craig was the charming and intelligent daughter of a Glasgow surgeon. When only 17 years old she married a lawyer.

Clarinda

The marriage was unhappy and four years later they separated.

After her father's death she and her children went to Edinburgh to stay with her cousin, Lord Craig at his house in York Place.

In December 1787 Nancy met Robert Burns at a Miss Nimmo's house in Alison Square, Potterrow, where she invited him for tea. The day before they were due to meet, Burns injured his leg and had to stay in his room for six weeks. During this time they wrote passionate letters to each other. Burns styled himself 'Sylvander' and she called herself 'Clarinda'.

On 13 January Clarinda wrote to Sylvander: 'last night was one of the most exquisite I have ever experienced . . . But though our enjoyment did not lead beyond the limits of virtue, yet, today's reflections have not been altogether unmixed with regret'.

Later they met more often but in 1791 for the last time. Burns wrote for her one of his most poignant songs:

Ae fond kiss, and then we sever;
Ae farewell, and then for ever!
Deep in heart-wrung tears I'll pledge thee,
Warring sighs and groans I'll wage thee.

Many years later (long after Burns had died) she wrote in her journal in her house at Calton Hill: 'This day I can never forget. Parted with Burns in the year 1791, never more to meet in this world. Oh, that we meet in Heaven!'

Now, walk forward, turn right towards the church and then glance left as you go. Here is the old Canongate Burgh Cross, central meeting-place of the people of the Canongate for gossip and trade.

Go to the wall of the church and you may hear a strong bass voice singing a folksong of Italy. Between the first and second windows is the uneven flatstone grave of the Italian musician and confidential secretary to Mary Queen of Scots **[18] DAVID RIZZIO** (also known as Riccio) c.1533-66.

Born in Turin, Riccio was the son of a musician. He first came to Scotland in 1561 as secretary to the Marquis of Moreto. When Mary Queen of Scots told the Marquis that she needed a bass singer for her chapel choir, he recommended Riccio. Shortly afterwards he was also made Mary's secretary.

Wishing to avoid her weak husband, Henry Lord Darnley, and caught between the demands of her Scots and French subjects, the Queen began to confide increasingly in Riccio – a relationship which caused much talk and envy among the Scots.

On 9 March 1566 the Queen, then expecting a baby, was dining in private apartments in the north turret at Holyrood with a few close friends when Darnley came into the room, followed by a group of armed men. They seized Rizzio, took him to another room, stabbed him 56 times and then threw his body down into the Palace courtyard.

Tradition has it that at the time of the Rebellion (1688) Riccio's body was taken from Holyrood and re-buried in the Canongate churchyard.

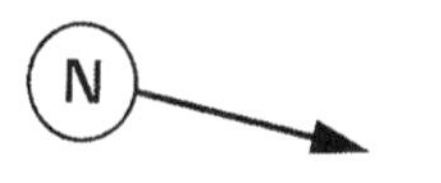

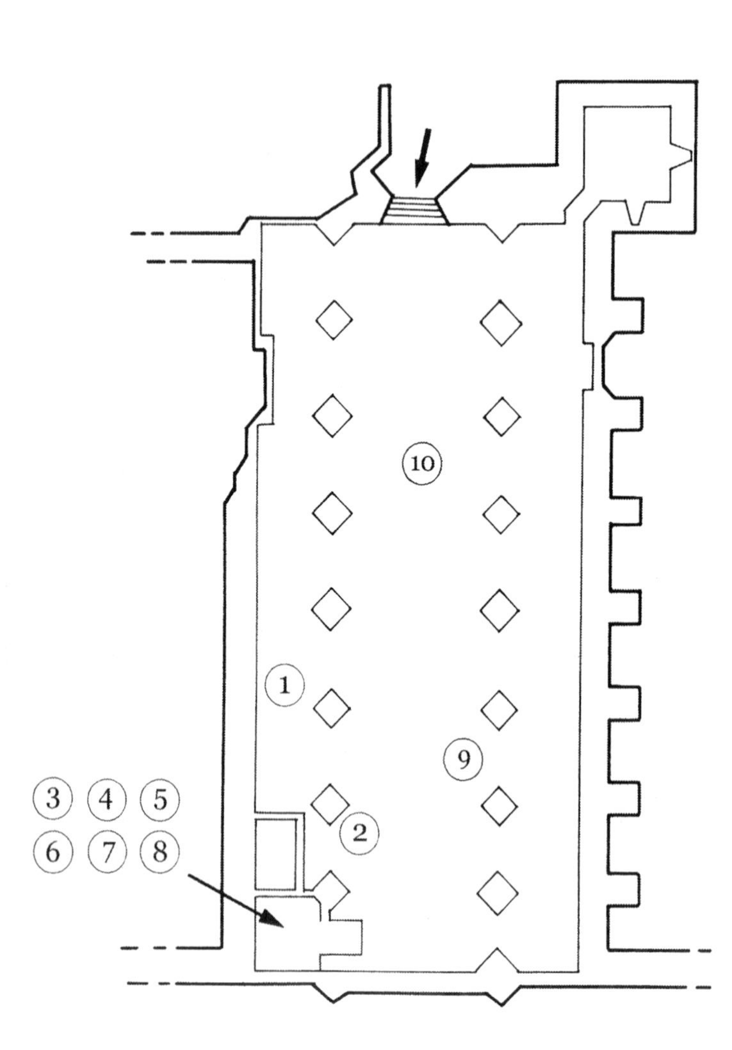

HOLYROOD ABBEY

Location – Abbey Strand

HOLYROOD ABBEY

Walking into the ruins of the Abbey church is an experience both moving and alarming. In 1780 the great Methodist preacher John Wesley recorded: 'The roof of the royal chapel is fallen in and the bones of James V and the once beautiful Lord Darnley are scattered about like those of sheep.'

The historian Hugo Arnot recalls events at the Revolution in the time of James VII, when the mob 'broke into the vault which had been used as the royal sepulchre in which lay the bodies of King James V, of Madaleine of France, his first Queen and of the Earl of Darnley and others of the monarchs and royal family of Scotland.

'They broke open the lead coffins, carried off the lids but left the rest. When we lately visited it . . . we found that what had escaped the fury of the mob at the revolution became a prey to the rapacity of the mob who ransacked the church after it fell in December 1768. In 1776 we had seen the body of James V and some others in their lead coffins. Now the coffins have been stolen.

'The head of Queen Madaleine which was then entire and even beautiful and the skull of Darnley were also stolen. His thigh-bones however still remain and are proofs of the vastness of his stature.'

In 1825 the antiquarian Charles Kirkpatrick Sharpe remembered 'many fragments of the royal bodies shown in the chapel of Holyroodhouse and a Countess of Roxburgh entire, saving one hand. The woman went into the vault and threw out the body on the grass – like a blackamoor's, with one white tooth which gave an undescribable horror to the face'.

To a later generation the Chapel was romantic, otherworldly. The composer Felix Mendelssohn, visiting Edinburgh in July 1829, observed that 'The chapel is now roofless, and is overgrown with grass and ivy, and the ruined Altar where Mary Queen of Scots was married. Everything is in ruins and mouldering, and the bright light of Heaven shines in. I believe I have found the beginning of my Scottish Symphony there today'. In his notebook he had written down the first 16 bars of his Symphony.

Marie, Duchess of Pomar and Countess of Caithness (1830-95), an over-imaginative lady at the best of times, wrote in her *A Midnight Visit to Holyrood*: 'Never could this once lovely chapel have looked more beautiful than it did

Holyrood Abbey

at this moment; instead of all the instruments that once resounded through its many arches, it was now pervaded by a still more solemn silence; instead of lighted torches and the innumerable wax tapers that once blazed upon its altars, it was now lighted alone by the stars of heaven, and these looked in upon me from all sides through each gothic window, and from the deep blue of the canopy that was my only roof.'

Stop at the main entrance to the church. Turn right and walk along between the free-standing pillars and the multi-coloured jigsaw stone wall, until you come to the fifth pillar. Under the second high window against the wall lies a long thin slab, the grave of **[1]** Sir **JAMES DOUGLAS** (1560-1608).

The life of Douglas was dominated by revenge. After the beheading of Regent Morton in 1581, Douglas attacked Captain James Stewart who had given evidence against Morton. He killed him, cut off his head and bore it away on a spear, leaving his body 'to be devoured by dogs and swine'.

Early on a July morning in 1608, Sir James was walking alone in Edinburgh's High Street when he was in turn attacked by a nephew of Captain Stewart. During the struggle, Douglas was stabbed to death.

Walk on to the second last freestanding pillar and go round it. High on its side, facing the centre of the church, is the stone commemorating **[2]** Bishop **ADAM BOTHWELL** (1527-93).

Bothwell had a foot in both the religious and secular world. Born in Edinburgh, he was appointed Bishop of Orkney in 1559. Soon after he became a Protestant and in 1563 was made a Lord of Session.

On 15 May 1567, at 4am, Bishop Bothwell married Mary Queen of Scots to the Earl of Bothwell according to the Reformed ritual (but it was rumoured that he had first married them according to the Roman rite).

After Mary's abdication, Bishop Bothwell crowned and anointed King James VI at Stirling, but by the end of the year the General Assembly called a debate on his conduct as an absentee bishop, an infrequent judge and a suspected Catholic sympathiser.

Bishop Bothwell, clever politician that he was, talked his way out of a corner. In 1570 he was appointed Bishop of Holyrood but again the Assembly complained that the 27 churches under the control of Holyrood were 'decayit and some made sheepfolds, and some sae ruinous that none dare enter, especially Holyrud Hous'.

Turn to your left and walk towards the end of the church. To your left is the Royal Vault. In earliest times the remains of all Royalty were buried in front of the High Altar. After the destruction of the monastery in 1544 and 1547 by the English army, only the nave of the church was left standing. The individual Royal tombs were emptied and the remains placed at the south-east corner of the new roofless chapel (around half the size of the original church), within a new Royal Vault. Here, these coffins lie silent, covered with purple cloth and studded with gleaming brass rivets shaped like flowers.

[3] DAVID II (1324-71), son of Robert the Bruce and the first king to be buried at

Holyrood, was married at the age of five to Joanna (the sister of Edward III of England). Shortly afterwards, Robert the Bruce died and David was crowned at Scone.

The young king never recovered from being thrust early into the limelight and Edward Balliol, supported by the English, claimed the Scottish throne. He defeated the Scots at Dupplin in 1332 and was crowned king. David and his queen were sent off to France for their own safety for seven years.

When he was 22 years old, David brought an army to England, fought like a lion but was defeated and captured by the Archbishop of York at Neville's Cross in 1346. He was held prisoner for 11 years until the Scots agreed to pay a ransom of 100,000 merks.

Hardened by this experience, David spent the rest of his life rebuilding Edinburgh Castle, constructing the 60 feet high King David's Tower. He also looked for ways of smoothing out relations with the English, but Scots still had heavy taxes to pay south of the

Holyrood Palace

Border. David married twice but had no sons and so his nephew, Robert II, succeeded him – the first Stuart king.

[4] JAMES II (1430-60), known as 'Fiery Face' due to a red birthmark, was born at Holyrood and became king at the age of six after the murder of his father, James I, in Perth. He was taken by his mother to Edinburgh Castle for safety and there held under house arrest by the Castle Governor until his mother smuggled him out, hidden on the back of a pack-horse.

Finally in 1449, James II took control of the kingdom, but the Douglases, in the person of the 8th Earl, continued to rival his power. James II gave the Earl safe conduct and met him at Stirling in 1452. He ordered the Earl to submit to him, but he refused. The King's men then stabbed Douglas to death.

As a ruler, James II was decisive and energetic but unpredictable. He built the first Edinburgh town wall and imported the giant cannon 'Mons Meg' to the Castle. At the siege of Roxburgh, James II was standing too close to a cannon. It exploded, killing him almost instantly.

[5] Queen **MARY of GUELDRES** (1433-63) was the daughter of the Duke of Gueldres in Holland. Mary, however, had spent most of her life at the sophisticated court of her flamboyant uncle Philip of Burgundy. In 1449 he put forward her name as a possible bride for King James III of Scotland.

She was only 16 when she landed at Leith, a charming, attractive girl. The Lord Provost of Edinburgh and 300 Scots soldiers led her to the monastery of the Greyfriars, set on a small hill surrounded by ornamental gardens.

Mons Meg

A week later she was married in the Abbey at Holyrood and reigned as Queen for 11 years. When James was killed at the siege of Roxburgh, she hurried to the scene and inspired the Scots to capture the castle. Then she took her young son quickly to Kelso and had him crowned king.

During the years when her son was too young to rule, Mary controlled Scotland with energetic efficiency; but she died suddenly in 1463. Behind her she left a good reputation for religious and social achievement.

She founded the Collegiate Church of the Holy Trinity (on the site of the present Waverley Station) in 1462. This was rebuilt in 1877 (much altered) at Jeffrey Street. Next to the Church was Trinity Hospital, which she also founded to 'house, clothe and feed seven destitute but worthy people'.

Over the centuries this number grew and the Hospital became the oldest Edinburgh charity (which still exists today). The building was demolished in 1845.

In the Scottish National Gallery at the Mound is the Holy Trinity altarpiece which gives us a clue as to the magnificence of the original church.

[6] JAMES V (1512-42) became King of Scotland when only one year old. At first his mother, Margaret Tudor, was Regent, then, when she married the Earl of Angus, it was the Duke of Albany who ruled Scotland in the name of the king.

During these unsettled years the two powerful houses of Hamilton and Douglas fought for control of the country. In 1520, 'Cleanse the Causeway' took place in the Cowgate, where the Douglases with over 500 men fought a merciless running battle with the Hamiltons through the narrow wynds and closes of the High Street. Around 80 of the Hamiltons died and so the Douglases under the Earl of Angus won the day.

In 1524 the Duke of Albany fled to France, James was put in the care of the diplomat Sir David Lindsay (author of *Ane Satyre of the Thrie Estatis*), but Angus took the King prisoner. James, however, escaped from Falkland Palace dressed as a groom and later took over the kingdom, asserting his authority, making sure his nobles obeyed him.

James believed strongly in social justice and from time to time would disguise himself in old tattered clothes and visit the homes of the poor to listen to their complaints. For this he was known as 'the Guidman of Ballangeich', the 'Gaberlunzie [beggar] King', the 'King of the Commons'.

After the death of his first wife, Madeleine, James married Mary of Lorraine who, aided by Cardinal David Beaton, began to persecute and burn the early Protestant Reformers at the stake. It was the execution of George Wishart in 1546 which resulted in widespread disgust in Scotland and led to the assassination of the hated Cardinal himself.

James V was a gifted poet, in many ways resembling the early promise and brilliance of his uncle, Henry VIII of England. He founded the College of Justice in 1532 and a magnificent window in Parliament House commemorates the event. However, after the defeat of the Scots by Henry VIII, at the battle of Solway Moss, James died of a broken heart.

[7] MADELEINE of FRANCE (1520-37) was the daughter of Francis, King of France (who entertained Henry VIII at the Field of Cloth of Gold in the year of her birth). She married James V of Scotland at Notre Dame Cathedral in Paris in January 1537 in the presence of kings and queens and the nobility of Scotland and France. At the banquet which followed, James gave the guests nuggets of gold mined from the hills of Scotland.

The Royal pair returned to Scotland in May 1537 accompanied by two French warships, bringing with them an enormous collection of jewellery, fine clothes and thoroughbred horses. They landed at Leith. As she stepped onto Scottish soil Madeleine bent down to kiss the earth, so endearing herself to the whole nation. She received a tremendous welcome and preparations were immediately put in hand for the coronation.

At this point Madeleine, whose health was not strong, took ill. Perhaps the rough Scottish climate was too much for her. She died 40 days after landing at Leith and was buried in Holyrood Abbey. Five years later James V died and was laid to rest beside his beautiful but tragic queen. They were the last king and queen to be buried in Scotland.

[8] Henry Stewart, **LORD DARNLEY** (1546-67) was born in Yorkshire. He was related to the English Royal family through his mother, Margaret Tudor, sister of Henry VIII. It was rumoured in 1560 that if Queen

Elizabeth of England died, the Catholics would try to have Darnley made king. It was then that Queen Elizabeth called for him. But although he cut a manly, sporting figure, and played the lute delightfully for her, he had no real strength of character and Elizabeth cunningly sent him northwards to her cousin, Queen Mary of Scotland.

Darnley arrived in Edinburgh in 1564. He met Mary and danced seductively with her. Persuaded that an alliance with Darnley would secure the English throne for Mary, they became betrothed. Their wedding on 29 July was no love-match but a marriage of political convenience.

It was not a successful union. Darnley drank heavily and was intensely jealous. Mary's Italian secretary, the charming singer David Riccio, was murdered in front of the already pregnant Queen by Darnley and his accomplices, Darnley's dagger being pointedly left in the corpse.

Darnley became an increasing embarrassment to Mary. He was indiscreet, sometimes betraying confidential state information and had allowed himself to be used by the powerful Scottish lords who already resented the foreign manners and tastes of their Queen.

When Darnley caught smallpox he was sent to the house of Kirk o' Field (where Edinburgh University Old Quad now stands). In the early morning of 10 February 1567 the house was blown up. Darnley and his servant were found in mysterious circumstances in a garden 40 feet away. There were no marks on the bodies but they seemed to have been strangled. To this day the true facts of the matter are not clearly established.

As well as the Royal adults buried in the Abbey, seven infant princes and three princesses were laid to rest there between 1430 and 1602: **Alexander** (born and died at Holyrood, 1430), the son of James I; **David** (1456-57) son of James II; **James** (1507-08), born at Holyrood, the son of James IV; a **daughter** of James IV, who died after baptism (1508); **Arthur** (1509-10), born at Holyrood, and a son of James IV; a **daughter** of James IV, who died after baptism (1512); **James** (1540-41), born at St Andrews, the son of James V; **Arthur** (born at Falkland, dying soon after birth in 1541) the son of James V; **Margaret** (born in Dalkeith but died soon after birth in 1598), the daughter of James VI; and **Robert** (1601-02), son of James VI.

For almost 500 years Holyrood was also the burial place for the ordinary people of the Burgh of Canongate, both inside the Abbey Church and in the churchyard. In 1685 James VII closed the churchyard, but burials in the Chapel Royal continued into the 18th and 19th centuries (for example, that of George Earl of Caithness in 1889).

Mysterious miniature coffins found NE of Arthur's Seat in 1836

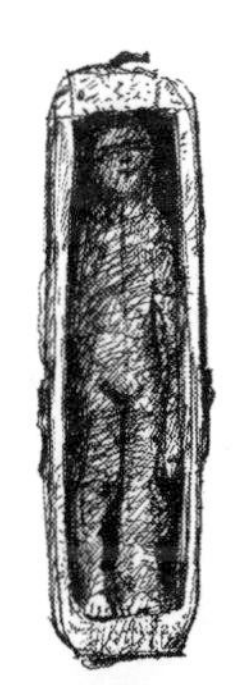

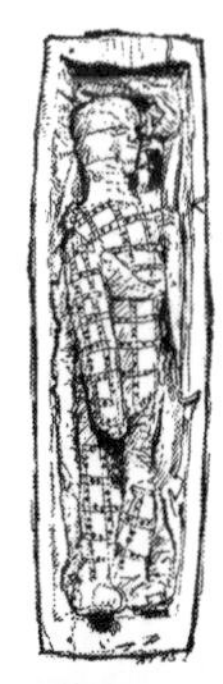

Now walk across the church towards the altar in the centre. It has two plain shields on the side facing you. This is the tomb of **[9]** Sir **JOHN SINCLAIR** (1754-1835), the editor of the *First Statistical Account of Scotland* (1791-98), compiled from information sent in by parish ministers all over the country.

He was also MP for Caithness, a member of both the Scottish and English Bar and founder of the British Wool Society (1791). He was the first President of the Board of Agriculture and in 1810 became a Privy Councillor. For his good works he was knighted. Then he set out on a long tour of Europe, later publishing details of his travels.

Turn back now to the entrance of the church by which you came in. Walk towards the ten white marble ovals set in stone on the ground. Go to the last one on the left. This is the grave of **[10] MARIE**, Duchess of **POMAR** (1830-95).

A high-born Spanish lady living in Paris, she married first a Spanish count and then the Earl of Caithness. She called her house in Paris 'Holyrood' and claimed she could communicate with Mary Queen of Scots (whom she idolised and said she had spoken to during a midnight visit to the Palace). As Countess of Caithness she had the right to be buried in the family vault at the Abbey.

As you leave the church, spare a thought for **[11] JOHN PATERSON** (1600-63), the location of whose grave is unknown. He was a shoemaker, a Canongate Bailie and also an expert golfer. When the Duke of York (afterwards James VII) was living in Holyrood in 1681, two English nobles claimed that golf had been invented in England. To prove their point they challenged the Duke to a game of golf with a partner of his own choice.

The Duke chose John Paterson, the finest golfer in the city, and in the game at Leith Links the Englishmen were thrashed. The Duke won a sizeable bet and as a reward for Paterson's help he is said to have given the stake money to Paterson who used it to renovate the family home in the Canongate at what is now known as 'Golfer's Land'. The shoemaker was also allowed to use a crest showing a right hand gripping a golf club with the motto *'Far and Sure'*.

Last of all, but not least, we come to **[12] DAVID RICCIO/RIZZIO** (1533-66), whose body was thrown out of a Palace window after his murder. The body of the Italian musician and secretary to Mary Queen of Scots was then taken first to the porter's lodge and placed on top of a chest. The porter's assistant is said to have remarked: 'Davie sleepit on this kist [chest] when he first cam here, an' at the end he lieth here again – a very ingrate and misknown knave'.

First the body was buried outside the south-west door of the Abbey on the left of the present entrance, so that people coming in and out of the church would walk over it. Later, when Mary returned to power, she had the body removed to the Royal Vault – but it is believed that it was finally taken back to the door of the church. Then it is thought it may have been re-interred outside the Canongate Kirk where a large marked stone now covers the grave.

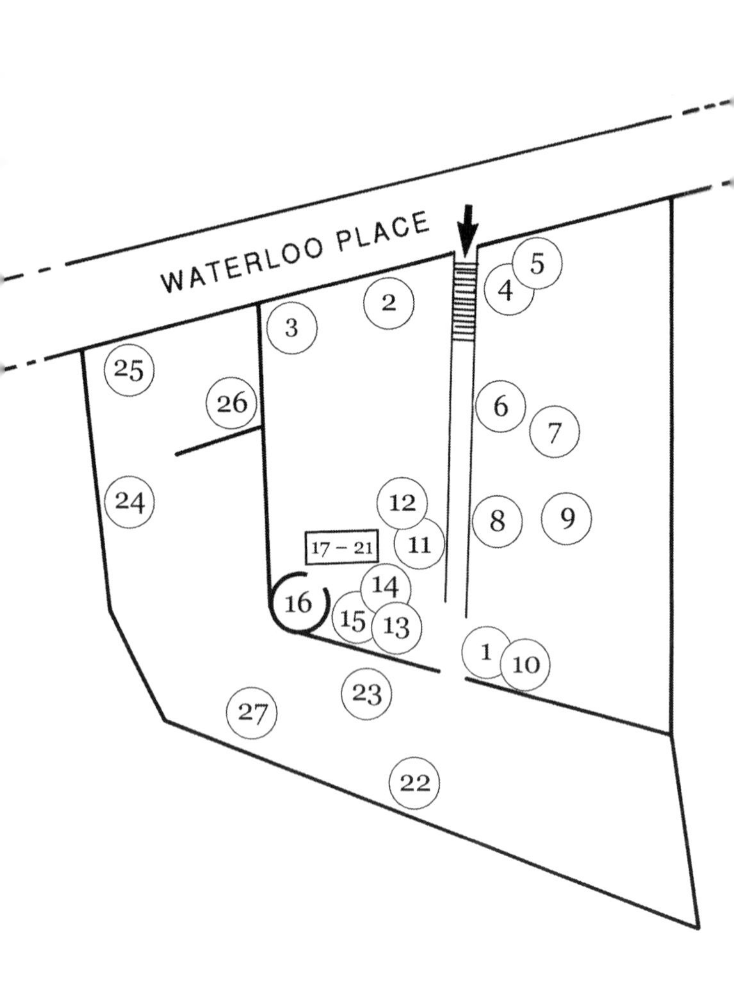

Old Calton Cemetery

Location – Waterloo Place

OLD CALTON

From the East End of Princes Street, walk past the sooty, salt-encrusted alcoves of Waterloo Place (on the south pavement) until you come to the black iron gate on your right. Enter the burial ground (note: visitors should take care not to visit this graveyard on their own at any time of day). The view that meets you looking up the steps is of the gigantic black obelisk, the **[1] POLITICAL MARTYRS** Monument silhouetted against the sky.

Pause for a moment to remember those brave and principled men who fought for electoral reform – the lawyer **THOMAS MUIR** (1765-98); the farmer **WILLIAM SKIRVING**; barrister **JOSEPH GERRALD**; and **THOMAS PALMER** (1747-1802), a Unitarian minister. **MAURICE MARGAROT** was the only one of the five men to return home alive from Botany Bay in Australia, dying penniless at the age of 70.

Looking up at the tall black monument pointing accusingly into the sky, you can

Political Martyrs

almost hear Thomas Muir speaking at the end of his long trial before the hated judge Lord Braxfield: '*When our ashes shall be scattered by the winds of heaven, the impartial voice of future times will rejudge your verdict*'.

The foundation stone of the 90-foot obelisk was laid in 1844. Dressed from head to foot in black, 400 members of the Complete Suffrage Association walked past Edinburgh's High Court and then covered the entire side of the Calton Hill with black, menacing in mourning. Robert Burns is said to have been so moved at the injustice done to of the Political Martyrs that he composed 'Scots Wha Hae' in their honour.

As you climb the steep steps from Waterloo Place, you emerge from street-level into the light of day. It is almost like rising from your grave on the Day of the Last Judgement! To right and left gravestones are shoulder-high. On the far right the gnarled stone drum of the David Hume monument immediately catches the eye, framing the bronze statue of a pensive President Abraham Lincoln. He stands tall above a freed black slave, weathered green but emerging from centuries of injustice. Up on the far left huddles what remains of the feared Calton Jail – the turrets of the old governor's house.

Today we have lost much of the elaborate panoply of death to which our ancestors attached so much importance. Imagine for a moment a funeral typical of the time of Sir Walter Scott who found the ritual cheap and offensive. He describes how 'the funeral pomp set forth – *saulies* (hired mourners) with their batons and *gumphions* (funeral banners) of tarnished white crepe. Six starved horses, themselves the very emblems of mortality, well cloaked and plumed, lugging along the hearse with its dismal emblazonry, creeps in slow pace towards the place of internment, preceded by Jamie the idiot who, with weepers (strips of muslin stitched onto the edges of the sleeves of his black coat) and cravat made of white paper, attended every funeral and followed by six mourning coaches filled with the company'.

At the top of the first set of steps turn back and look over the road for a moment to what is left of the rest of the burial ground after Waterloo Place was constructed, the road driven through the east end of Princes Street to Regent Road. Some gravestones are still visible there, left beside what was once the main entrance to the burial ground.

Now climb the second set of steps to the pink- chipped pathway, stepping to the right and then walking back over the grass towards Waterloo Place. Near the retaining wall is one of the gravestones of local Calton tradesmen who once filled the district with bustle and noise. The inscription reads: 'Here lyes the body of **[2] THOMAS MYLNE**, Smith in Calton, who died on the 12th June 1770 aged 31 years'. At the top of the stone you can see the crown of honour and the hammer of his trade (metal-worker and tin-smith).

Turn left towards the far-off statue of the Duke of Wellington on his prancing horse.

Thomas Mylne

The facing wall holds the imposing monument to **[3] JOHN MORTON** (*d.*1739 aged 61), fashionable hat-maker in the burgh of Calton. On top is the face of an angel framed by its wings – this is the so-called 'winged soul' – the soul departing the body at the moment of death. On each side are two plump topless women holding up a book – symbolising the fruitfulness of the Word of God. For Morton, trade and piety went very much hand in hand, but there is also an under-current of sex-appeal!

Go back in the direction you came and cross over the central path to the other side, walking towards the same wall over Waterloo Place. Look at the picturesque headstone of **[4] ELIZABETH WILKIE** (*d.*1747) and **[5] THOMAS GRAY** (*d.*1732), wright (carpenter) in a busy Pleasance workshop. At the back of the stone are a square and compass – the symbols of Freemasonry.

The stone was erected by their son, seafaring Captain John Gray, and shows a full-masted galleon (with castles on its three masts) straining in the wind, carving a foaming wake through the heaving ocean. Below are three-dimensional thigh-bones, a skull, a monstrous bearded male head and that of a woman wearing a wide lace collar – these are probably the masonic emblems of the sun and moon. Also carved delicately into the stone is a small anchor. You can almost smell the salt sea-spray.

Turn back up the grass slope towards the Martyrs obelisk, passing to the left a sunken crowned winged head mouthing softly the message *Memento Mori* ('Remember you too will die'). Luxuriant laurel bushes and rampant ivy cover many of the walled graves behind.

Now we come to three thespians – perhaps you can smell the grease-paint or hear the sound of applause not far away in the old Theatre Royal in the former Shakespeare Square (the building later demolished to make way for what became the General Post Office), clapping echoing over long-demolished rows of seats?

To the right is the rear of the pink granite slabstone of **[6] JAMES LUMSDEN** (1836-99), couthy singer of Scots songs whose annual Lumsden Burns Festivals packed the Usher Hall year after year with fans eager to hear the old traditional melodies and enjoy a nostalgic whiff of the Highlands and Borders.

Catch behind you the sonorous tones of the tragic actor **[7] WILLIAM WOODS** (1749-1802) who trod the creaking boards at the old Theatre Royal in many a stirring leading role, tugging at the heart-strings. In the audiences which thrilled to his art were the poets Robert Fergusson and Robert Burns who became Woods' devoted friends.

Notice also the inscription on the back of the stone lamenting that 'the animated graces of the player can live no longer than the instant breath and motion that presents them'. How they would have valued a video camera to capture the actor's skill for posterity!

Then comes the grey granite obelisk to **[8] CHARLES MACKAY**

John Morton

(1787-1857), yet another gritty star of the old Theatre Royal. Mackay was a character actor who caused a sensation in 1819 as Bailie Nicol Jarvie in Sir Walter Scott's *Rob Roy*. Scott was bowled over by Mackay's performance – 'he seemed to bring more out of it than I ever put in. I was electrified by the truth, spirit and humour which he threw into it'. It almost seems as if the candles on the now-darkened stage still flicker in his memory.

Just before you reach the Martyrs Monument you pass on your left the square, eight-foot-tall pillar commemorating members of the Williamson family. You will know you are there by the muffled but blood-curdling Red Indian war-cry in the air, for beside the pillar lies the body of **[9] PETER WILLIAMSON** ('Indian Peter'), 1730-99. Kidnapped from the pier at Aberdeen when only eight years old, he was sold into slavery in Philadelphia. Despite having been scalped by Red Indian tribesmen, he used his knowledge of survival in the wild to escape and joined the army to fight against the Indians.

The old Theatre Royal in what is now Waterloo Place

David Allan

When he retired to Edinburgh (scalped bald head and all), he opened a popular tavern and coffee-house beside St Giles and soon moved into book-selling, printing and publishing. He set up the first Penny Post and brought out the first Edinburgh street directory (1773). Indian Peter was one of the most famous, argumentative and colourful figures in town, always ready to tell a hair-raising tale of life on the run.

Can you smell a mysteriously attractive scent where you are standing? To the left of the base of the Martyrs obelisk is the handsome Greek temple grave of the elegant perfumer **[10] WILLIAM RAEBURN** (*d.*1812) who must have sent many a young Edinburgh belle into the town's dancing assemblies on the sweetest of breezes.

Face right, looking towards the statue of Abraham Lincoln. To the far left is a fine view of Edinburgh Castle; hard to your right through a gap in the buildings you can see out past Leith, over the Firth of Forth to the hills of Fife.

Straight in front of you, over the top of the slabstone of **[11] THOMAS WHYTE** (a Calton baker), with its whiff of warm loaves early in the morning, is a round white plaque with the profile of the historical painter **[12] DAVID ALLAN** (1744-96). Born so tiny that he had to be wrapped in cotton-wool, he grew up to win the St Luke gold medal in Rome for composition and became director of the prestigious Edinburgh Trustees Academy, a forerunner of the Edinburgh College of Art.

Beside him is the grave of a shoemaker (*d.*1762), identifiable by its symbols of a crown above a half-moon knife, recalling the smell of cut and polished leather and the ding of the hammer.

Walk back a little and step down onto the central path. Go forward towards the Political Martyrs Monument. Just before you reach their obelisk turn right up the four little steps to David Hume's monument, passing the walled grave of **[13] ALEXANDER REID** (*d.*1788). In front of you is the tablestone of **[14] ROBERT HOLMES**, a Belfast merchant who died on a visit to the city in 1808.

Go left round the Hume monument to the boundary wall and look south over to the Royal Mile. You are at the grave of **[15] WILLIAM GIBSON** (*d.*1807), Assistant Superintendant of Mail Coaches – 'The bright example of a generous mind' – whose vehicles clattered in and out of the city in wind, rain and shine, bringing packets, parcels, love-letters and bills.

You are now beside the **[16] DAVID HUME** (1711-76) monument based on the design of the tomb of the barbarian Theodoric the Great in Ravenna, Italy. Theodoric eventually brought peace to Italy through religious toleration. The monument (by Robert Adam) is open to the elements much like a roofless Scottish 'broch' with a single fragile tree sprouting leaves behind the iron spikes and bars of the gate. It is designed as a tribute to a man who was a warm-hearted friend, sympathetic and kind, but who could not bring himself to accept the existence either of God or of an after-life. He was victimised for his benevolent atheism by the dogmatic church and town authorities of his day who blocked his appointment to all Edinburgh University teaching posts.

Towards the end of his life Hume lived between Princes Street and St Andrew's Square at No 21 South St David Street. One morning his maid went out and found that one of his friends had chalked 'St David's Street' on the side of Hume's house. She went in to tell her master fearing he would be furious but Hume's laconic answer was merely 'Never mind, lassie, mony a waur man has been made a saint o' before!'

Hume and Lincoln

Groundless rumours that Hume had made a pact with the Devil were taken so seriously by his many friends that, after his funeral, they kept a constant watch over his grave, eight of them guarding the tomb every evening, firing pistols and lighting lanterns placed on the grave. They kept this watch up for eight nights after his internment.

Standing 15 feet above the turf is the commanding life-size figure of the American President Abraham Lincoln (the first statue of him to be erected in Europe), freeing the black slave who sits below among the flags of battle, lifting his hand in gratitude.

Here also are the graves of five Scotsmen who died in the American Civil War (1861-65), in the smoke and noise of battle, far from the land of their birth – **[17]** Sergeant Major **JOHN McEWAN** of the 65th Illinois Volunteer Rifles; **[18]** Lieut. Col. **WILLIAM DUFF** of the 2nd Illinois Artillery; **[19] ROBERT STEEDMAN** of the 5th Maine Infantry Volunteers; **[20] JAMES WILKIE** of the 1st Michigan Cavalry; and **[21] ROBERT FERGUSON** of the 57th New York Infantry Volunteers.

Return to the central path and go beyond the base of the Political Martyrs Monument towards the Royal Mile. Facing you is the iron-studded door of **[22] DANIEL STEWART**'s tomb, the founder of Daniel Stewart's Hospital. Stewart (1741-1814) worked at the Scottish Exchequer in Parliament Square for 43 years and died unmarried. But he never forgot those less well off than himself (he was born into poverty in Perthshire). With the money that he left

Daniel Stewart's Hospital (now Stewarts-Melville College), designed by David Rhind, was built in Queensferry Road.

Turn right down the granite-chipped path. Beside you on the right is the flat stone which marks the final resting-place of **[23] JULIUS VON YELLIN**, an unfortunate member of the Royal Academy of Munich. He was 'seized with illness' while addressing the Royal Society of Edinburgh at the Royal Institution (now the RSA building at the foot of the Mound). He went to his bed in the Royal Hotel and never got up again. Sir Walter Scott attended von Yellin's funeral on 24 January 1826 – his first public act 'after the great misfortune of his life' (his bankruptcy).

Walk on down and following the path as it bears right below the back of the David Hume monument. As you go down on to the grass you will see in front of you to the left the unmarked walled grave of the sculptor, **[24]** Sir **JOHN STEELL** (1804-91), its black iron cage ('mortsafe') bursting with spotted yellow laurel bushes and a vigorous fig-plant, an ancient and redundant gas light-fitting jutting above your head.

Steell was responsible for most of the finest statues in Edinburgh – Alexander taming Bucephalus (1832) now in the City Chambers; the seated figure of Queen Victoria on top of the Royal Scottish Academy (1844); Sir Walter Scott under the Scott Monument (1840-46); the Duke of Wellington on horseback (1852); the first Viscount Melville in Melville Crescent (1857); Allan

The Iron Duke, in bronze, by Steell

Ramsay above the Floral Clock (1865); John Wilson in Princes Street Gardens (1865); Dr Chalmers in George Street (1878) and Prince Albert on horseback in Charlotte Square (1876). Queen Victoria was so pleased with her recently deceased husband's statue that she knighted Steell at the Palace of Holyroodhouse.

Ironically, every trace of John Steell has been erased from his grave – the once-locked gate swings open, the wall where an engraved plaque once was is now scarred and pitted by the elements. The man who spent most of his working life making monuments to others has no recognisable memorial to himself. His is a grave with no name.

Facing you further on in a quiet leafy corner is the elaborate grave of the publisher, **[25] WILLIAM BLACKWOOD** (1776-1834), town councillor and founder of the Tory *Blackwood's Magazine*, which only ceased publication in 1976. From his august premises at 25 George Street, Blackwood published many of the finest writers in what was affectionately known as 'Maga' as well as other works, including the *New Statistical Account* (1840). On each side of the black ornamental gate torches flame upside down in mourning.

Turn to your right and under the ivy you see on the far wall the bronze profile of another great Edinburgh publisher, **[26] ARCHIBALD CONSTABLE** (1774-1827), tall, bluff and hearty, the genial open-handed bookseller who published the *Scots Magazine* from 1801, bought up the *Encyclopaedia Britannica* and published the works of Sir Walter Scott. After moving into a new shop at No 10 Princes Street Constable planned to serialise Scott's 'Waverley Novels' but in 1826 his London agents went bankrupt, dragging Constable with them and in turn ruining Sir Walter. Constable's life ended in ill-health and bitter disappointment.

In a walled tomb to the south of the cemetery is the grave of **[27] THOMAS REID** (1746-1831). One of the great Scottish clock-makers, Reid was born in Fife and came to Edinburgh to serve his apprenticeship before going to London. There he worked for 11 years before returning to Edinburgh to set up his own business in Parliament Close, off the High Street. In 1809 Reid moved his premises to Princes Street and expanded his production of eight-day grandfather clocks, specialising in the installation of astronomical regulators. Among them was the clock in the Calton Hill Observatory which was used for dropping the time-ball on the Nelson Monument.

As well as making clocks for churches such as St Andrew's in George Street (1788) and reconstructing others (for example, that of St Giles in 1797) Reid wrote *On Clock and Watch Making,* which was to become the standard work of its time. For his achievements Reid was elected an Honorary Member of the Worshipful Company of London Clockmakers.

Several other burials of note are in unmarked graves. Along with Allan Masterton and William Nicol, **[28] WILLIAM CRUICKSHANK** (*d.*1795) was one of three High School masters who were friendly with the poet Robert Burns. A graduate of Edinburgh University, Cruickshank was rector of the Canongate School before taking up an appointment in 1772 as one of the teachers of Greek and Latin at the High School in Infirmary Street, Edinburgh.

Burns stayed with Cruickshank at his house in No. 2 St James Square and it was to Cruickshank's daughter, Jenny, that he wrote his 'A Rose-bud by my early walk'. When Cruickshank died in 1795 Burns wrote an 'Epitaph for Mr W. Cruickshank':

Honest Will to Heaven's away,
And mony shall lament him;
His fau'ts they a' in Latin lay,
In English nane e'er kent them.

In an unmarked grave east of the obelisk to the Political Martyrs lies **[29] WILLIAM NICOL**. Nicol was born near Annan in Dumfriesshire into a working-class family. His native intelligence and hard work, however, enabled him to secure a place at Edinburgh University where he studied medicine and theology and in time also became a teacher of Greek and Latin at the High School. Sir Walter Scott, who was at that time one of his pupils, says that 'Nicol was an excellent classical scholar, but worthless, drunken and inhumanly cruel to the boys under his charge.' Nevertheless, three of Burns' closest friends in Edinburgh were masters at the High School and Nicol was the closest of the three.

In August 1787 Burns lodged at Nicol's home for almost three weeks and took the quick-tempered dominie with him on his tour of the Highlands later that year, comparing himself to 'a man traveling with a loaded blunderbuss at full cock'.

In the autumn of 1789, Nicol, Burns, and another of the High School masters, Allan Masterton, got together. During their celebrations, Burns wrote his well-known drinking-song 'Willie brew'd a peck o' maut', referring to Nicol's homemade whisky (written to a tune composed by Masterton):

O Willie brew'd a peck o' maut,
And Rob and Allan cam' to pree;
Three blyther hearts, that lee-lang night,
Ye wad na found in Christendie.

(Chorus)
We are na fou, we're nae that fou,
But just a drappie in our e'e;
The cock may craw, the day may daw,
And ay we'll taste the barley bree.

By 1795 Nicol had retired but still taught privately near what is now Cockburn Street. He died in Merchant Street off Candlemaker Row, aged 53.

Leave the Old Calton Burial Ground. If you are curious, cross the road and take the first turning to the left down Calton Hill. Turn first left again. Climb the steps and in front of you is the other section of the Old Calton Burial Ground.

Having satisfied your curiosity, return to Waterloo Place and cross over to the former government buildings at St Andrew's House. Go past the entrance to Calton Hill, below the black telescope of Nelson's Monument. To your left is the former Royal High School. In front of you are the green slopes of Arthur's Seat and the jutting angle of Salisbury Crags.

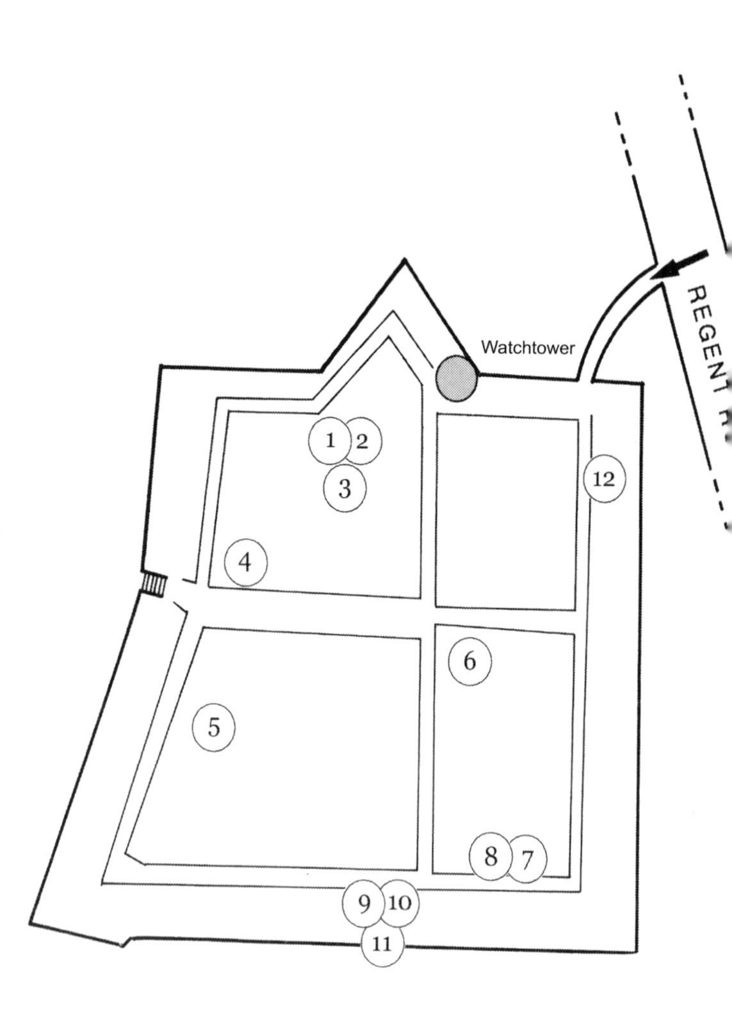

New Calton Cemetery

Location – Regent Road

New Calton

Walk on down towards the Burns Monument which commands a view of the Firth of Forth. Beyond the Monument turn right down into the New Calton Burial Ground.

If Old Calton lies high above the heads of the passers-by, then New Calton does the reverse – it falls away as you enter, a long sloping field. As you go in you see on your right the boarded-up watch-tower. From the gate there is a good view of Holyrood Palace with its roofless Abbey and gold-tipped turrets and the new Scottish Parliament.

Turn right towards the watch-tower. When you get there, turn to face the Firth of Forth where it opens into the North Sea. Walk forward ten paces down the right side of a low wall. Do you hear the wail of a distant bosun's whistle or the crack of canvas flapping in the wind or the groaning of ship's timbers? New Calton was once known as 'the cemetery of the admirals' – at least five are buried there: for example, **[1]** Rear Admiral **ANDREW SMITH** (*d.*1831, aged 65). Follow the line of graves to your left – the second is that of **[2]** Vice Admiral **ALEXANDER FRASER** (*d.*1829) and **[3]** Vice Admiral **THOMAS FRASER** (*d.*1870, aged 74).

Walk on over the grass to reach the path. Turn right and walk down it. At the end of the wall to your right is the red granite stone of gruff **[4] DAVID BRYCE** (1803-76), architect of the Royal Infirmary, Fettes

College and the Bank of Scotland headquarters at the Mound. Bryce worked right up to his death from bronchitis.

Walk on down the path again towards the Canongate, down to the bottom of the steps and turn left. Just before reaching the large tree turn back left again up he slope.

On your right is the broken white pillar marking the honoured grave of **[5] ANDREAS GREGOROWICZ**, a Polish lawyer, surgeon, soldier and freedom-fighter who died in 1838 aged 31. Having fought against the Russians, he escaped to Edinburgh where he began training as a surgeon. Within a year he was dead from the plague, contracted while he attended the city's poor.

Continue back up the slope. When you reach the path again turn left and then first right at the next intersection. Walk up the slope for ten paces – on your right is the red granite headstone of the farrier **[6] WILLIAM DICK** (1793-1866) born in White Horse Close beside its coaching-stables. Dick understood

New Calton

animals and made them his life. He developed the discipline of veterinary science in Edinburgh and founded the Dick Veterinary College, becoming a Professor of the University of Edinburgh in 1844.

Walk on to the end of the path and at the T-junction turn right. Walk down to where the path turns right under a large tree at the far end of the burial-ground and follow it. Immediately on your right is the fine red granite stone of **[7] WILLIAM MacGILLIVRAY** (1796-1852), Professor of Natural History in Aberdeen and author of *A History of British Birds*. At the bottom of the stone is a bronze plaque of the King of Birds – an eagle waiting for its prey, full of power and noble aggression.

Beside it, by contrast, is the grave of poor **[8] ROBERT MACKERTER** who spent 50 years in the service of the Earls of Haddington and died in 1841 aged 78 ('*Zeal, Fidelity and Attachment*'), self-effacing by nature and by trade.

The fifth walled grave to your left has the smell of the sea. Here lie **[9] ROBERT STEVENSON** (1722-1850) and his sons **[10] THOMAS** (1818-87) and **[11] ALAN** (1807-65). Robert Stevenson, grandfather of Robert Louis Stevenson, studied engineering and worked for the Northern Lighthouse Board, overseeing the construction of 20 lighthouses, shining beacons

Robert Stevenson

over the cruel sea, through fogs and through storms. He invented the intermittent and flashing light, so much a feature of the modern lighthouse.

His greatest achievement was the Bell Rock Lighthouse laboriously constructed on a dangerous reef in the North Sea. Stevenson also had great influence on the future shape of Edinburgh – he engineered Waterloo Place, supervised the construction of London Road, designed the Calton Jail, drained the Nor' Loch to make Princes Street Gardens and planned Granton Harbour.

His son Alan built 10 lighthouses, including the Skerryvore 14 miles into the Atlantic. Thomas Stevenson, father of Robert Louis, was also a specialist in lighthouse illumination.

The visit to New Calton cemetery now over, turn back uphill towards the gate. Just before you reach the gates spare a glance to the right at the square pillar with its crudely-carved skull and cross-bones, the grave of **[12] JAMES STRACHAN**, a humble tanner sweating in his reeking dye baths at Canonmills.

James Strachan

As you exit by the gates, pause at the elaborately-decorated shoemaker's grave with winged soul in free flight, winking skulls, scrolls, juicy bunches of grapes and the familiar sly whispered message – *Memento Mori.*

DEAN

The gnarled pillars of the main gate, with pyramids balanced on top, the glimpse of trimmed green-and-gold holly bushes mixed with ancient yews reveal that you have arrived at the most elegant of all Edinburgh's cemeteries.

But the elegance was achieved at a cost – writing in 1845, Lord Cockburn (later to be himself buried here), records his horror at the savagery of the construction gangs who built the cemetery: 'I thought that venerable trees and undying evergreens were exactly what a burial-ground would long for. Here they are in perfection – plenty hollies and yews, apparently a century old; and how did I see these treated? As a drove of hogs would treat a bed of hyacinths!'

As you pass through the heavy black gates turn first left and then first right. Walk past nine Celtic crosses (white, pink and grey granite). On your left is a glorious wilderness – birds sing in the treetops and below is the valley of the Water of Leith, a secret river fringed by the spires of churches pointing skywards.

Continue along the path until you see a large pink granite pillar on your right with a green bronze classical head on

David Octavius Hill

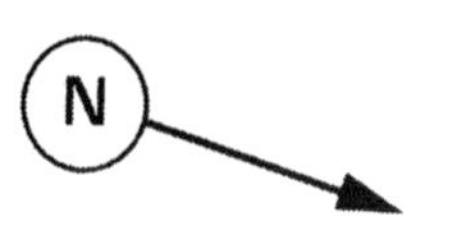

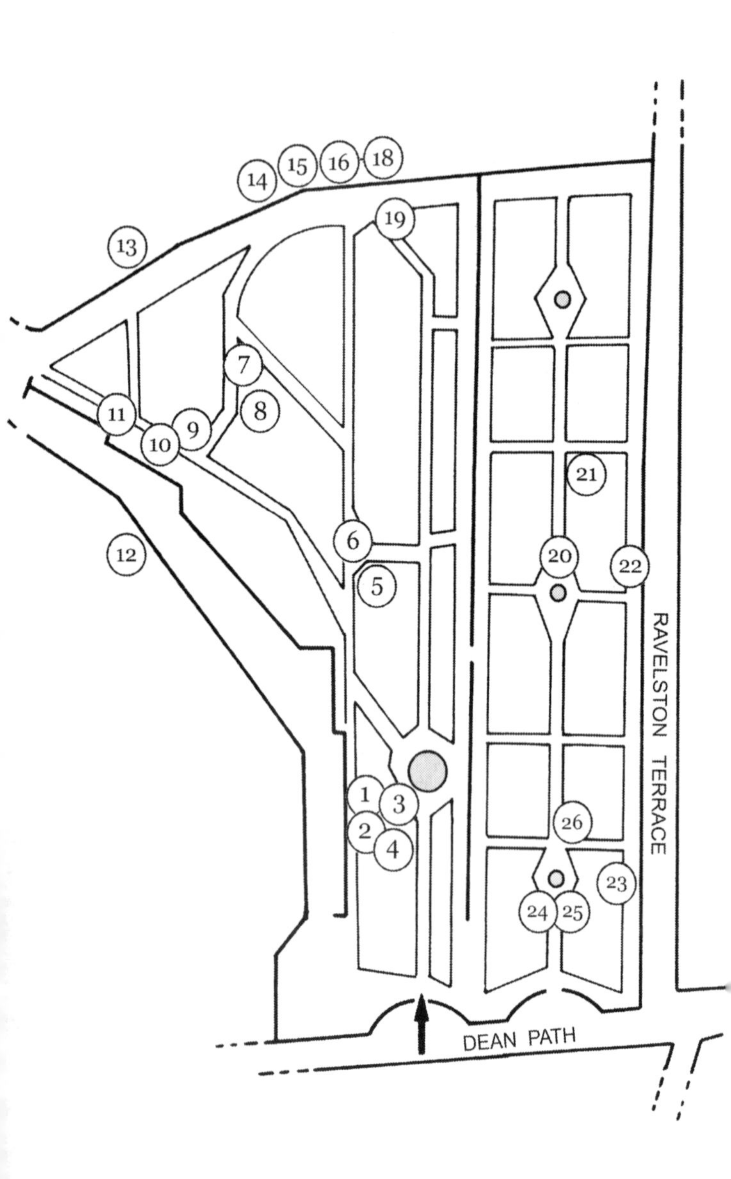

Dean Cemetery

Location – Dean Path

top, its eyes stained black, its beard flowing. This is the grave of two fine artists – **[1] DAVID OCTAVIUS HILL** (1802-70) the photographic pioneer, and his second wife **[2] AMELIA ROBERTSON PATON** (1820-1904) the sculptor who lovingly fashioned the bronze head of her famous husband in the costume of a Roman emperor.

Imagine the soft click of the shutter on Hill's camera or the agony of his sitters who had to pose stock-still for minutes on end, their heads and arms locked by invisible metal clamps. See how the sun dazzles his eyes as he squints through the antique lens?

Hill (originally a painter), worked with his associate Robert Adamson on the flat roof of his home at Rock House on the Calton Hill taking 'sun-pictures' (*calotypes*) and in the fishing villages by the Firth of Forth, making atmospheric portraits with the new chemical mysteries of photography. His own masterpiece was a giant painting of *The First General Assembly of the Free Church of Scotland* (1843-66), studies for which he made using portrait photographs. Among the public sculptures by his wife is the figure of David Livingstone the explorer, which stands beside the Scott Monument.

Now walk to your right over the grass to the tall Celtic cross, with fantastic animals woven together in perfect symmetry. Designed by his brother William, it commemorates the painter **[3] DAVID SCOTT** (1807-49),

David Scott

who trained in Italy, like so many Scottish artists. His green bronze head above the cross weeps a long black tear. Scott, a brilliant but unfashionable painter, lived a lonely and embittered life in the family home of Hermits and Termits at St Leonards, wracked by mental illness.

Close by is the grave of **[4] ROBERT ANSTRUTHER** (1823-95) doctor, Arctic explorer and traveller who sailed in 1849 looking for the ill-fated Franklin Expedition. Again, in the following year, he took part in the continued search organised by Lady Franklin. On the monument you see five men straining at a sled with dogs pulling another. Behind is their three-masted ship the *Advice* surrounded by mountains of ice and snow. Can you hear the howl of the Arctic wind and the creaking of the ice, can you feel the frost-bite at your fingers and the pangs of a terrible hunger?

Return to the path and walk quickly on. Trimmed into enormous dark living monuments yew and holly trees tower ominously above you. Peep over the parapet wall to your left. There is the Water of Leith slipping between knotted and twisted trunks. Make towards the black obelisk in front of you.

As you approach it, just before the second path leading to the right, you can catch your breath in front of the stylish headstone to the artist **[5] SAM BOUGH** (1822-78). Below the bronze portrait-head, with grizzled beard and Bohemian neck tie is a

Sam Bough

bronze palette, brushes and oil-paints, the tools of his trade.

Now walk to the foot of the enormous obelisk dedicated to the six officers and 369 NCOs and men of the **[6] 79th HIGHLANDERS** who died in Bulgaria and fell in the Crimean War (1854-55) at the battles of Alma and Sevastopol. Also commemorated are five officers and 343 NCOs who died in India (1857-71).

Continue past the obelisk and take the first turning on the left. Walk forward until you reach another large blunt obelisk on your left with the name of the Covent Garden tenor **[7] JOHN WILSON** (1800-49) carved on it. Wilson's bronze profile has long side-burns and curly hair.

Turn left round the obelisk and go along the path which gradually curves towards the right. On your left is the tall red sandstone Celtic cross commemorating members of the Chambers family, including the Peebles-born publisher and historian, **[8] ROBERT CHAMBERS** (1802-71). Together with his older brother, William (1800-83), he founded W. & R. Chambers and went on to become one of the world's leading publishers. Robert, a prolific writer of reference publications, also made important contributions to Scottish history such as his *Traditions of Edinburgh* (1824) and *A Biographical Dictionary of Eminent Scotsmen* (1832-34).

When you reach the T-junction look right. Suddenly the ground begins to tremble and strange eastern music fills your ears with unease. A weird grey pagan carving looms at you like a bad dream – three winged lions

John Leishman

under three rams' heads, and a column above surrounded by three pelicans, ending in a shallow dish high above – it looks ready for a ritual sacrifice. This is the unsettling gravestone of **[9] JOHN LEISHMAN** (1801-61), Writer to the Signet and **[10]** Brigadier-General **OFFLEY SHORE** (1866-1922).

Gather your thoughts together quickly. Immediately on your left across the path is the simple modest headstone of **[11] HENRY D LITTLEJOHN** (1826-1914), the city's first Medical Officer of Health (1862) who dramatically reduced the cases of typhus and smallpox in the city. Dr Littlejohn was the man responsible for a *Report on the City Cemeteries* (1883) and lectured on medical jurisprudence at Edinburgh University from 1856.

Henry Littlejohn

Continue up the path past a weeping woman sheltering by a spotted laurel bush with her elbows on an urn. Ignore her pitiful cries. Take the first almost hidden path to your left and walk down between holly and rhododendron for 100 paces. At the second angle of the wall on your left is a magnificent Celtic cross, the last resting-place of the painter of fairies and medieval mystery, **[12]** Sir **JOHN NOEL PATON** (1821-1901).

Turn back and retrace your steps. As

you reach the top of the path, again walk straight forward towards the large pink granite pyramid in the distance.

Ten plots on is the white marble monument to **[13] ALEXANDER MONRO** *Tertius* (1773-1859), the last in a dynasty of grandfather, father and son who collectively held the Chair of Surgery in Edinburgh for 125 years. Monro *Tertius* was not, however, a particularly exciting teacher – he used to read from his grandfather's lecture-notes word for word! [*see Greyfriars churchyard for Monro Primus and Secundus*]

Nineteen plots further on is the grave of the lawyer **[14] HENRY COCKBURN** (1779-1854) with Gothic stonework and bronze profile. Cockburn defended Thomas Burke's wife in the Burke and Hare Resurrectionist trial of 1828, helped to draft the first Scottish Electoral Reform Bill, founded the Edinburgh Academy and the Commercial Bank and was Solicitor General for Scotland.

Alexander Monro *Tertius*

He loved nature and the environment and is best summed up by *The Edinburgh Review* (to which he often contributed), as 'rather below the middle height, firm, wiry and muscular, inured to active exercise of all kinds, a good swimmer, an accomplished skater and an intense lover of the breezes of heaven. He was the model of a high-bred Scotch gentleman. He spoke with a Doric breadth of accent. Cockburn was one of the most popular men north of the Tweed'.

Henry Cockburn

The Cockburn Association, active in preserving and enveloping what is best in Edinburgh's heritage, is named after Henry Lord Cockburn. Among his descendants were the journalist Claud Cockburn and the novelist Evelyn Waugh.

Next to it is the plain white altar to the architect **[15] WILLIAM PLAYFAIR** (1789-98) who designed many of Edinburgh's best-known buildings – the National Gallery, the Royal Scottish Academy (both at the Mound), the National Monument on Calton Hill and Surgeons' Hall.

A surprise is the arresting pink granite pyramid to **[16] ANDREW RUTHERFORD** (*d.*1852) and his wife **[17] FRANCESCA**.

Beyond is the raised table-altar to **[18] FRANCIS JEFFREY** (1773-1850), Lord Advocate and founder of the influential *Edinburgh Review* (1802) at his Buccleuch Place flat. While a student

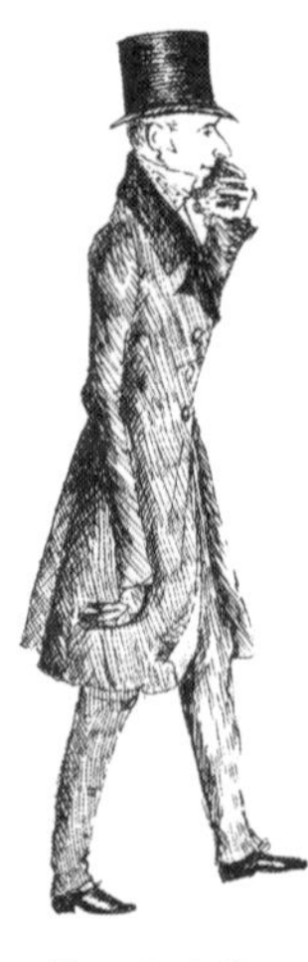
Francis Jeffrey

at Oxford, Jeffrey once carried a drunken James Boswell (the biographer of Dr Johnson), up to his room.

Walk forward till you meet a dark green Celtic cross which tells the moving story of **[19]** Lt **JOHN IRVING RN** (1815-1848/9) who left England with the explorer Sir John Franklin in May 1845 on the HMS *Terror*, in an expedition to find the North West Passage to the Pacific Ocean. They wintered at Beechey Island and then sailed south down Franklin's Strait, entering the North West Passage. For two years they were locked in the ice. Sir John Franklin, other officers and 15 seamen died – on the monument we see two ships, 15 men, some leaning wearily on shovels and a number of sleds. The 105 survivors (Lt Irving among them) landed on King William's Land and tried to march into Canada but all died from cold and lack of food. They were so hungry that they had begun to eat the corpses of their dead companions.

After 33 years, Lt Schwatka of the American Searching Expedition discovered Irving's grave. His remains were returned to Britain and buried in the Dean cemetery in 1881. Carved into the cross is a bronze relief showing the Franklin Expedition on the ice. Today the sun shines warmly on it.

Continue to the end of the path where it meets the far wall. Turn right and walk along to the opening in the wall to your left.

Go through the wall, turn left and then first right. Walk towards the gigantic pink obelisk to **[20] ALEXANDER RUSSEL** (1814-76), one of the editors of *The Scotsman*.

Elsie Inglis

Turn left and walk to the end of the enclosure; on the right, at the corner, is the gravestone of suffragette, surgeon and reformer **[21]** Dr **ELSIE INGLIS** (1864-1917). This Indian-born founder of the Scottish Women's Hospitals for Foreign Service, served in Serbia, the Ukraine and Romania during the First World War, organizing medical care in Russia even in the chaos of the Revolution.

She founded a maternity hospital in Edinburgh in 1902 and in 1906 founded the Scottish Women's Suffragette Federation. Even after her death Dr Inglis was the inspiration for a number of hospitals opened in her name, notably the Elsie Inglis Memorial Maternity Unit (1925-88) in Edinburgh. For her work in Serbia she was given the highest national award, the Order of the White Eagle, with the commendation that 'Scotland made her a doctor but Serbia made her a Saint'.

Return to the Russel obelisk. Go round it on the right and continue straight towards the boundary wall. As you reach the T-junction at the wall look slightly left at the white marble cross facing you, the grave of **[22]** Dr **JOSEPH BELL** (1837-1911), the inspiration for Sir

Joseph Bell

Arthur Conan Doyle's world-famous detective Sherlock Holmes.

As a young medical student at Edinburgh University Conan Doyle was astonished at the deductive powers of his lecturer, Dr Bell. In 1892, Doyle wrote to his former teacher: 'It is most certainly to you that I owe Sherlock Holmes, although in the stories I have the advantage of being able to place him in all sorts of dramatic situations'.

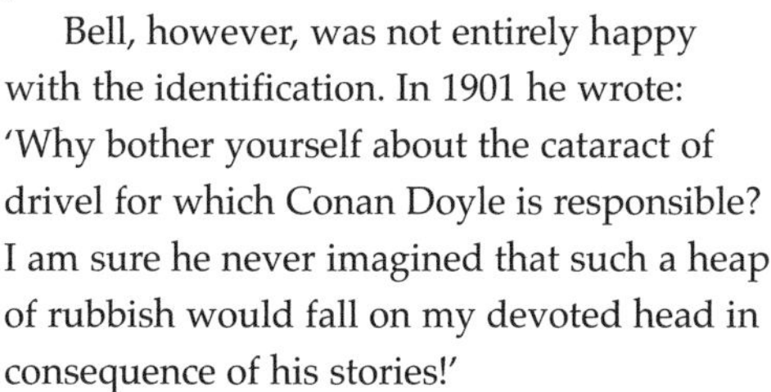

Bell, however, was not entirely happy with the identification. In 1901 he wrote: 'Why bother yourself about the cataract of drivel for which Conan Doyle is responsible? I am sure he never imagined that such a heap of rubbish would fall on my devoted head in consequence of his stories!'

The *Strand Magazine* (in which the Holmes stories first appeared), quoted Conan Doyle as saying of Bell: 'His intuitive powers were simply marvellous.'

Appointed early in life as Surgeon to the Royal Infirmary, Dr Bell retired and was then made the first Surgeon to the Sick Children's Hospital (then in Morningside Drive). He was a familiar figure driving to and from work in his carriage.

Sherlock Holmes

Now turn right down the path along the wall. Shortly before the end of the path, on your right is a large dark green obelisk with a bronze bust of **[23]** Major General Sir **HECTOR MACDONALD** (1853-1903), a figure of mystery, a soldier so brilliant that he was rumoured to have risen from the dead!

'Fighting Mac' was born in Easter Ross, the son of a crofter. Enlisting as a private in the 2nd Battalion the Gordon Highlanders, he rose rapidly through the ranks to become a colour sergeant.

During the Afghan campaigns he performed spectacular acts of bravery and leadership, and was offered the choice of a Victoria Cross and a comfortable life as an NCO, or a commission with little income. Despite the financial hardship, exacerberated by the expense of life in the officers' mess, Macdonald chose the commission and began an equally meteoric rise as an officer of outstanding ability.

He married at Edinburgh Castle and subsequently was transferred to South Africa where he distinguished himself against the Boers and virtually saved the whole British army at the Battle of Omdurman.

It was this last achievement which, it is alleged, antagonised the future General Kitchener and led to the unhappy chain of events which ruined Sir Hector's career. In dubious circumstances, he was accused of homosexuality while in service in Ceylon.

On his way to London to answer the highly publicised charges, he booked into a Paris hotel and was found soon afterwards in his room shot through the head – apparently suicide.

In great secrecy, his coffin was taken to the Dean cemetery – even the horses' hooves were muffled – and buried at night.

Rumours, however, began to circulate that the Paris suicide was *not* the Major General and that his coffin had been weighted only with stones. For, by a curious coincidence, his distant cousin Colonel von Mackensen of the Prussian army had died on the very same day in a Berlin military hospital.

Months afterwards it was announced that a terrible mistake had been made – Colonel von Mackensen (the German form of 'Mackenzie') was not dead after all; he had only been seriously ill and had lost his memory. He was able to speak German but only with great difficulty.

Was Mackensen really Sir Hector Macdonald? Popular gossip thought so. Certainly, from this time on von Mackensen seemed suddenly to develop rather extraordinary military skills and by the end of the Great War had risen to the rank of Field Marshall and then to Commander-in-Chief of all German and Austrian armies at the Eastern Front.

Many years later, during the 1936 Berlin Olympics, von Mackensen, an ancient mustachioed officer wearing a bearskin Hussar cap with the skull and crossbones, was to be seen seated next to Adolf Hitler. So the mystery of 'Fighting Mac' remains a tantalising possibility.

What cannot be disputed is the strength of popular feeling. On the first Sunday after his funeral a huge pilgrimage began to his tomb which continued for some months afterwards. Even today, a weathered strip of green and yellow tartan is often

Hector Macdonald

seen tied round the base of the bust, knotted around a sprig of heather.

Shake off that eerie feeling and continue quickly down the path following it as it turns right. As you reach the locked gates on your left turn right up the broad path towards the tall Celtic cross. This is the monument to the Nasmyth family, a steam-hammer on one side and on the other the sword and broken hammers of the family crest.

Both **[24] PATRICK NASMYTH** (1787-1831) and **[25] JAMES NASMYTH** (1808-90) and their wives are buried here. They were sons of the famous painter Alexander Nasmyth (who is buried in St Cuthbert's).

Patrick Nasmyth followed his father's trade and became a landscape painter of note, fathering six daughters, all of whom were artists. James Nasmyth, 'engineer, astronomer and artist' as the monument describes him, helped to finance his studies at Edinburgh

The Nasmyths

University by selling model steam engines which he made at a small brass foundry in his bedroom.

Aged 19, he designed and built a steam car which ran up and down the Queensferry Road carrying eight passengers. He also invented a steam-blast and a dinner oven, the profits from which allowed him a fairly comfortable existence.

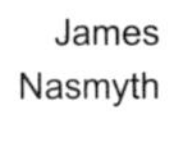
James Nasmyth

In 1834 James Nasmyth established his Bridgewater Factory at Manchester and six years later designed his famous steam-hammer, which played such a key role in the Industrial Revolution. After his retirement in 1856 he turned to astronomy, designing and manufacturing telescopes.

Walk forwards towards the Russel obelisk again. The ninth grave on your right is that of the oceanographer **[26]** Sir **JOHN MURRAY** (1841-1914). Born in Canada of Scottish parents, he went to Edinburgh University, first as a medical student, but then studied a wide variety of subjects – chemistry, law, natural history and literature. At 27 he spent six months as a surgeon on a whaler and worked on Jan Mayen Island in the Greenland Sea. Later he joined the Challenger Expedition to the Antarctic and edited the results of the Expedition, becoming director of the Challenger office in 1876 at Challenger Lodge (now St Columba's Hospice).

Murray was not only a marine zoologist but a pioneer of modern oceanography. He surveyed the Scottish freshwater lochs. He also helped to found the Millport biological laboratory and the Ben Nevis Observatory.

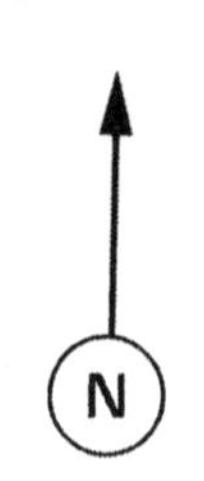

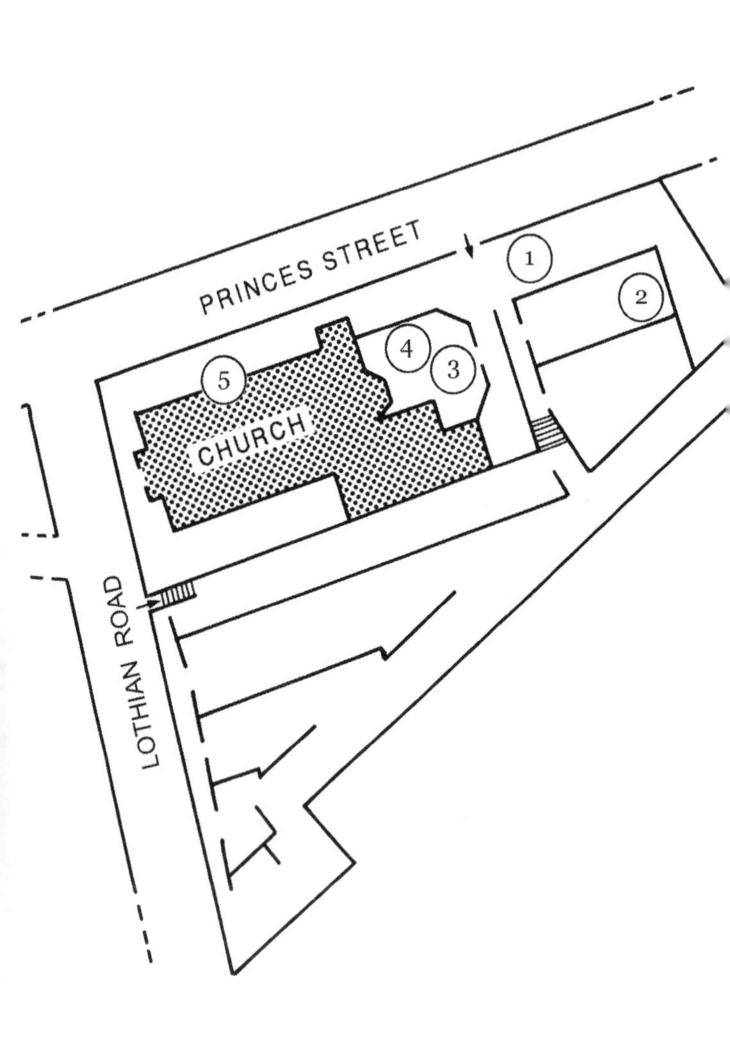

St John's Churchyard

Location – Princes Street / Lothian Road

St John's

You enter the grounds of the Episcopal church of St John the Evangelist (at the West End of Princes Street) through the gate opposite South Charlotte Street. There you pass by on your left the magnificent white Celtic cross erected in memory of **[1]** Dean **EDWARD RAMSAY** (1793-1872), one of the few people to have a memorial paid for by public subscription.

The Dean was a well-loved figure, a fine flute-player, an expert on the mysteries of campanology (bell-ringing) and a financial wizard who presided over the administration of St John's for 44 years.

Ramsay's *Reminiscences of Scottish Life and Character* preserve for posterity a fund of anecdotes of city life and valuable examples of the Scots tongue.

Edward Ramsay

Walk down the slope for a few feet and then bear sharp left into a burial enclosure. On the far right set into a low wall almost hidden from view is the red granite stone of **[2] JAMES SYME** (1799-1870), known as the 'Napoleon of Surgery', the greatest surgeon of his day, who trained and practised in Edinburgh. One of his

James Syme

house-surgeons vividly describes the working life of this Professor of Clinical Surgery: 'Two lectures a week, operations two days more, a ward visit when he wished to see any special cases. He spent generally about two hours in the hospital . . . In his little room where he at once took up his post with his back to the fire and his hands under the flaps of his swallow-tail coat . . . he generally held a small levée of assistants, old friends, practitioners wanting to arrange a consultation, old pupils home on leave. Before this select class, he examined each new and interesting case that could walk in. The new cases had been collected, sifted and arranged by the dresser in a little room on the stair, irreverently known as the "trap". Mr Syme then and there made his diagnosis, which to us young ones seemed magical and intuitional, with certainly the minimum of examination or discussion. One was sent off with a promise of a letter to his doctor, another was fixed for tomorrow's lecture or next day's operation.'

Syme was a popular lecturer with 'students racing to get to the nearest seats in the large operating theatre'.

Go back the way you came. Walk up the slope and turn left up to the 'Dormitory' garden attached to the back of the church. Facing you is the small white stone to **[3] ANNE RUTHERFORD** (1732-1819) – Sir Walter Scott's mother. She was an Episcopalian, while his father (buried at Greyfriars Kirk) was a member of the Church of Scotland).

Henry Raeburn

Now walk to your right. In the middle of the wall, smothered in summer with white and yellow roses, is the grave of **[4]** Sir **HENRY RAEBURN** (1756-1823), son of a yarn-boiler. His father died when Raeburn was only six and he was sent to Heriot's Hospital. After his schooldays he was apprenticed to a goldsmith and jeweller in Parliament Square.

One day the well-known seal engraver David Deuchar came to the shop and noticed the young apprentice quickly hiding something he was working on. It turned out to be a copy of a miniature painting which had been sent in for repair. Deuchar was so impressed by Raeburn's work that he engaged him to make more. Deuchar also introduced Raeburn to the painter David Martin who helped him in his study of art – Raeburn's only formal training.

Raeburn's elder brother had taken over his father's business in Stockbridge and it was in that part of the city that Raeburn met the Countess of Leslie, Ann Edgar, whose husband had recently died. He painted her portrait and fell in love with her. They married and Raeburn settled into a comfortable life as a man of means at Deanhaugh.

Heriot's Hospital

Raeburn, now with the wherewithall to develop his talent, travelled to London and then Rome to broaden his outlook; on his return to Edinburgh he built his own studio at York Place.

Raeburn's method of working has been recorded by a sitter: 'He spoke a few words to me in his usual brief and kindly way and then, having placed me in a chair on a platform at the end of his painting-room in the pose required, set up his easel beside me with the canvas ready to receive the colour.

'When he saw all was right, he took his palette and his brush, retreated back step by step, with his face towards me till he was almost at the other end of the room. He stood and studied for a minute more, then came up to the canvas and without looking at me worked on it with colour'.

Raeburn had a very orderly and regular life. He had breakfast at eight and was in the studio ready for his first sitter by nine, taking three or four sitters every day, painting each for around two hours.

Although bankrupted in 1807 by the failure of a family business, Raeburn owned a considerable amount of land and built Raeburn Place, Ann Street and Leslie Place (both named after his wife). Knighted by George IV at Hopetoun House in 1822, Raeburn died the following year after catching a chill on an archaeological expedition to Fife with Sir Walter Scott.

In his lifetime Raeburn painted over 600 portraits. He was also a man of wide-ranging interests in mechanics, archaeology, golf, gardening and archery. As Robert Louis

Stevenson was later to comment, Raeburn's great gift was to 'plunge at once through all the constraint and embarassment of the sitter and present the face, clear, open, and intelligent as at the most disengaged moments'.

Finally, enter St John's Church by the main west door and turn left to the stained glass windows. There you will see a brass plaque commerating the heroic **[5] JOHN STUART FORBES** (1849-76). A younger brother of Sir William Stuart Forbes of Pitsligo and Monymusk, he left Scotland under a cloud and emigrated to America. There, he changed his name to John Stuart Hiley and enlisted in the United states 7th Cavalry. At the Battle of Little Big Horn in Montana, 25 June 1876, along with nearly all the men of his Company, he died, under the onslaught of Sioux and Cheyenne Indians. The attackers stripped the soldiers of their uniforms, leaving no identification, and so the dead were buried anonymously in a common grave.

St John's Church, St Cuthbert's and the Castle

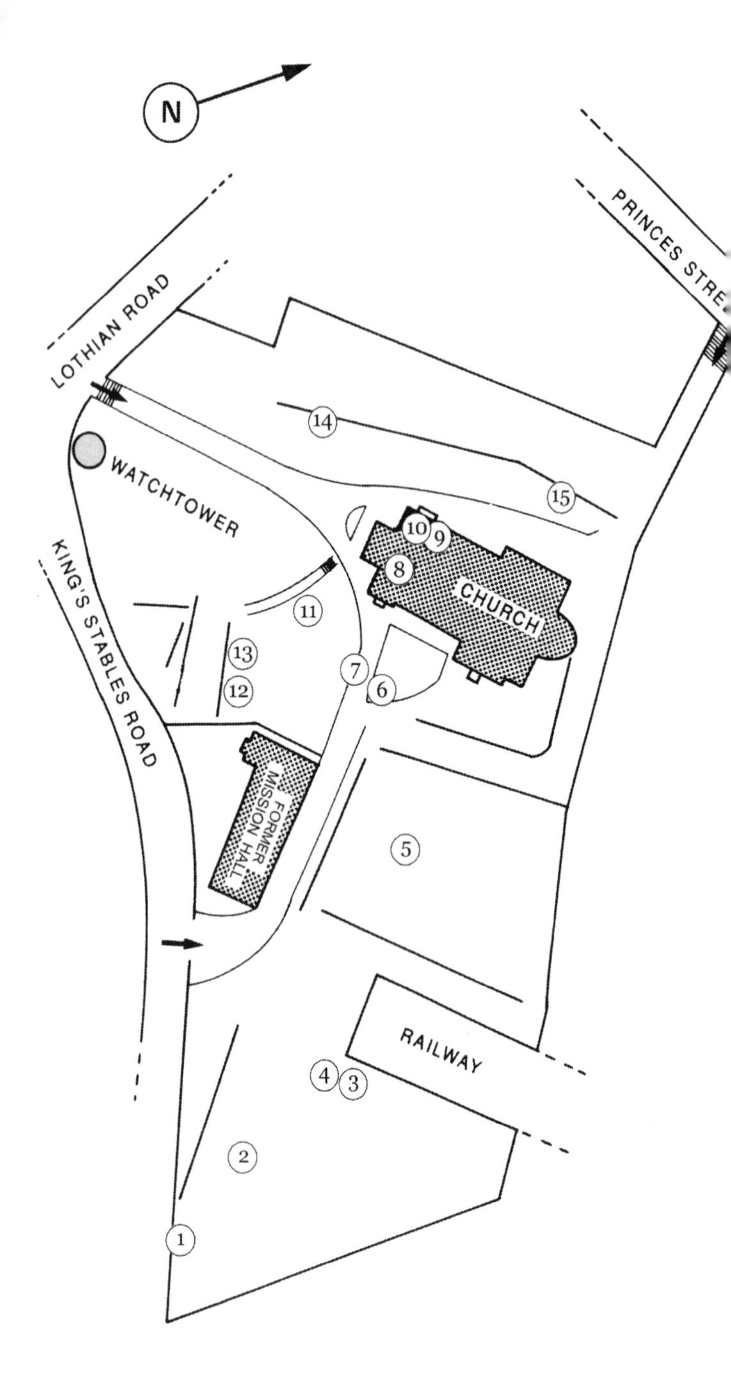

ST CUTHBERT'S CHURCHYARD

Location – Lothian Road/Princes Street

ST CUTHBERT'S

The site of St Cuthbert's Church has been holy ground since the Dark Ages. St Cuthbert (635-687), born in East Lothian, was a monk at Melrose and later Bishop of Lindisfarne. Tradition has it that he came up from Melrose, pitched his tent in the hollow ground below the Castle and so gave his name to the first church built outside the walls of the fortress.

The original St Cuthbert's was the mother-church of chapels at Liberton, Corstorphine and Boroughmuir, and a number of convents. After the Reformation it was renamed the 'West Kirk'. In 1774 a new church was built over the many earlier foundations and in 1789 a tower and spire were added over the burial-ground of the old West Kirk.

In the churchyard there are no pre-Reformation monuments – the first mention of a graveyard came in 1595 when the small hill to the south-west of the church (the 'Knowe'), which previously had been used to graze sheep, horses and cattle, was enclosed by a stone wall.

The original church had been sited on the 'Knowe'. The northern graveyard was added in 1787 and further additions were made in 1831 and 1834. In 1841 the Edinburgh and Glasgow Railway drove a cutting and a tunnel through the churchyard.

Being so far from the safety of the Old Town, St Cuthbert's was an easy target for the

'Resurrectionists' (or corpse stealers). In 1738 the problem became so serious that the walls of the churchyard were raised to eight feet. Two years later the Kirk Session appointed an officer to keep records of the dead and a lodge on the site of the present watchtower was used as an office for the 'recorder'.

But grave-diggers were still being bribed to leave the gates of the churchyard unlocked. Long after sunset you could glimpse dark, motionless figures driving silent carriages rapidly through the night.

When a number of bodies were stolen in 1742, the prime suspect was one of the Beadles. A mob of outraged citizens ran to his house and burnt it down.

In 1803 a regular watch was organised to patrol the churchyard at night. In 1827 a watchtower was built at the south-west (a little late in the day, as changes in the law would mean that the theft of dead bodies ended about ten years later).

St Cuthbert's Church

But there were some more fragrant treasures to be found. After part of the church collapsed in 1772, the building was demolished and a lead coffin was discovered. It contained some bones and a sweet-smelling lead urn which in turn held a human heart embalmed with spices. The church authorities pronounced that it was the heart of a soldier who had died in the Holy Land during the Crusades.

Enter by the west gate from King's Stables Road, turn half right and go diagonally to the end of the wall nearest you, which runs from the small lodge to your right, parallel to the boundary wall. Walk past the last grave on the wall-end (James Millar), and turn right along it. Follow the wall from the grave of John Forrester to the 24th monument where, under a tall street-lamp, lies **[1]** Mrs **ANNE GRANT** of Laggan (1755-1838).

Anne Grant lived at the end of Loch Ness inside the high bastion walls of the military stronghold of Fort Augustus where her father was barrack-master. In 1779 she married the minister of Laggan who was also the Fort chaplain. After 20 years of marriage, he died, leaving her with eight children.

Her time in Laggan, deep in the central Highlands, close to the River Spey, was well spent. She learnt Gaelic and investigated the language and customs of the Highlands. The romantic Scottish scenery is lovingly described in her *Letters from the Mountains*, written during her 30 years there.

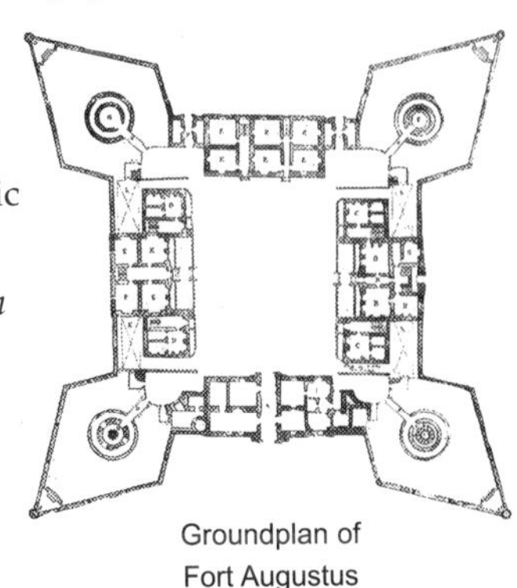

Groundplan of Fort Augustus

In 1810 Mrs Grant moved to Edinburgh where she stayed until her death.

Now trace your steps back again. At the eleventh grave on your right is the large Celtic cross dedicated to **[2] ALEXANDER NASMYTH** (1758-1840) who was born in the Grassmarket in the shadow of the Castle.

As a boy he loved clambering up the steep south side of the Castle Rock. His early years were spent at Edinburgh High School, after which he was apprenticed to a coach-builder. He soon showed his artistic talent, painting the side-panels of the finest carriages, and he took further art training at the Trustees Academy. Then Nasmyth was hired by Allan Ramsay, the portrait-painter, to work in London colouring-in backgrounds and painting the clothing in portraits.

He returned to Edinburgh in 1778 where he constructed his own house and studio at 47 York Place.

Nasmyth helped Patrick Miller, a wealthy banker with a bent for engineering, design a steam-driven boat and in 1788 they tried out the prototype on Dalswinton Loch with Robert Burns on board. One of Nasmyth's best-known portraits is that of Robert Burns.

Nasmyth helped design Thomas Telford's Dean Bridge and also drew up plans for the dazzling Temple of Hygeia over St Bernard's Well close to the Water of Leith. He was best known for his 'bow and string' bridge which was used all over Britain.

Nasmyth's elder son Patrick was also a painter known as 'the father of Scottish landscape'; his youngest son James became the inventor of the steam-hammer.

Now turn towards the railway cutting in front of you on the right. Under the trees you see the tall monument to the lawyer **[3] ROBERT JAMESON** (1784-1834), a sculptured memorial by Sir John Steell in the Greek style showing a young man protecting a child from a mysterious threatening figure behind.

Jameson's skill as a lawyer and his honesty made him one of the leading figures of his day in the Scottish courts. But his early death meant that his promise was never fulfilled. The Faculty of Advocates paid for the handsome monument as a mark of their respect.

On the other side of the monument is the grave of Robert's father (although with a different spelling of the surname) – **[4]** Revd **JOHN JAMIESON** (1759-1838) who holds a special place in Scottish history for having preserved much of our traditions and language in his *Etymological Dictionary of the Scottish Language* (1808-09).

Jamieson was not a minister of the Church of Scotland but a Dissenter (an *Antiburger*), like his father. He was the first Seceder to be awarded a Diploma of Divinity from the College of New Jersey, USA.

One of Jamieson's first charges as a minister was at Cowal, Argyll, where he often preached in the open air. 'For my canopy I had a pair of blankets stretched on two poles. The situation was sufficiently romantic for the sea flowed behind and the mountains of Argyllshire completed the view. In spite of the weather I never addressed a more attentive congregation or one more devout.'

Dr Jamieson lived in Edinburgh's George Square but was always fond of fishing outside the city. In later life he was prone to bilious attacks and was forced to tour all the Scottish spas to take the waters. Tragically, before he died, Dr Jamieson lost his wife and 14 children, one after the other.

Now go towards the black street-lamp at the rear of the former Mission Hall beside the gate you came in by. Just before you get there turn half right into the large grassy enclosure. Walk 32 paces into the centre of the grass. Here is the tall monument to **[5] GEORGE MEIKLE KEMP** (1795-1844), the shy, brilliant designer of the Scott Monument whose own coffin was accompanied by over 1,000 mourners.

Kemp had begun life as a shepherd which gave him time to pursue his hobby – making model mill-wheels. Later he trained as a carpenter near Peebles and as a mill-wheelwright. In his spare time he studied the construction of the great Border Abbeys and created designs for a reconstruction of Glasgow Cathedral.

Kemp's death was a tragedy which came out of the blue. On the evening of 6 March 1844 he had gone to visit the contractor for the Scott Monument at his office beside the Union Canal Basin at Fountainbridge to check on the supply of stone. Kemp left the contractor and set off down the tow-path along the Canal – a favourite walk of his.

The night was foggy and dark and he lost his bearings, took the wrong path and fell off the pier near the Lochrin Distillery into the icy waters of the canal. Although an expert swimmer, he seems to have been sucked down into the deep mud at the bottom.

It was a week before his body was found. A thorn walking-stick was the first clue to appear. Then his hat floated to the surface – he always wore it securely attached by a cord to his coat – and so the body was discovered.

Rumours now began to spread that he had been drunk or had committed suicide or that some jealous rival in the Scott Monument competition had attacked him. But there was no evidence for any of this.

It was expected that Kemp would be buried under the Scott Monument but this proved to be impossible. Today George Meikle Kemp lies with a view of his masterpiece through the trees across Princes Street Gardens.

Walk towards the door of the church now, out past the wall surrounding the central enclosure you have been in. As you emerge, you see on your right a triangular plot of ground shaded by a large weeping tree. Facing you is a sandstone obelisk. Listen to the music of the organ, for this is the grave of **[6]** Revd **ROBERT SMITH** (1780-1829), composer of the hymn 'How beautiful upon the mountains', former choirmaster of Paisley Abbey and musical conductor of St George's Parish Church.

Can you hear the soft sighing of a distant violin?

The Scott Monument

Perhaps it is because you are close to the memorial stone of **[7] GIROLAMO STABILINI** (1761-1815), violinist and teacher. His grave is at the level of the path, set into the retaining wall to your left.

Born in the hot back-streets of Rome, Stabilini came to Edinburgh in 1783, a talented young man invited by the directors of the Musical Society of Edinburgh, who were anxious to find a suitable new leader for their orchestra. Stabilini brought with him his Guarnerius violin and soon became undisputed king of the Edinburgh concerts.

His violin concerto, played during the interval at the Theatre Royal in front of George IV in 1822, became a favourite with the King who was seen in his box drumming his fingers in time to the music.

The Italian threw himself into the city's social life. He joined the Freemasons, the Royal Edinburgh Volunteers and liked to go to Leith Races, on one occasion injuring his precious 'bowing-arm' there. He was open, friendly and happy-go-lucky, with a taste for good wine and was liked as much by the ordinary Edinburgh resident as by the noblity in whose houses he played.

Robert Burns, a fellow Freemason, also attended a number of Stabilini's concerts and evidently enjoyed them.

Stabilini's career was, however, being affected by his enjoyment of the good things in life. He died of dropsy and his friends carried his body out of his Rose Street lodgings feet first.

Set at the base of the retaining wall his headstone is topped by a Roman harp with the Latin inscription that, to the great sorrow of his friends and admirers at his early death, Stabilini's violin now 'lies silent'.

John Napier

Go to the main door of the church. On the back wall to your right is the magnificently-carved stone monument to **[8] JOHN NAPIER** (1550-1617), with musical cherubs and bulging with ripe fruit.

Napier was born at Merchiston Castle (now the centerpiece of Napier University at Colinton Road). His father was Master of the Scottish Mint. Born in the year which saw the birth of the Scottish Reformation, Napier studied at St Andrews and travelled widely on the Continent.

He was fascinated by astronomy, mathematics, alchemy and astrology and even had a reputation as a wizard because of his uncanny understanding of the natural world. However, Napier kept himself very much to himself. He was often to be seen

Merchiston Castle

walking in the evenings dressed in a long cloak and accompanied by his large black dog.

Despite his reputation, Napier was a staunch supporter of the Reformed Church, throwing himself with tremendous energy and imagination into theology and science. He was a Commissioner for the Presbytery of Edinburgh at the General Assembly (1588), and in 1593 he published *A Plaine Discovery of the Whole Revelation of St John*, strongly critical of the Roman Catholic Church.

Napier is better known, however, for a series of practical military, industrial and agricultural inventions – for example, a tank; a powerful mirror for setting fire to ships at sea; artillery capable of firing in every direction; a hydraulic screw for clearing flooded mine-workings; and a variety of new methods of farming .

But it was his invention of Logarithms in 1617 (a technique of calculation using rods or bones carved with numbers) which made him an outstanding figure in the history of mathematics, an early pioneer in the development of the computer and one who helped lay the mathematical foundations that made the 1750 Industrial Revolution possible.

Standing in the church you may catch a whiff of scent on the air, hear the rustle of silk and a woman's musical laugh. Near you, close beneath the memorial plaque to **[9]** Sir **JAMES ROCHEAD** (1666-1737) halfway up the far staircase in the church, is the burial-place of **[10]** Mrs **JANET ROCHEAD** (1725-90), one of the most elegant women in Edinburgh.

Janet Watson of Muirhouse married Alexander Rochead in 1750 and went to live in the family home of Inverleith House (the present Royal Botanic Garden), with its avenue of trees and shaded glades. Within five years her husband died.

She is remembered with amazement by Lord Henry Cockburn – 'she would sail like a ship from Tarshish, gorgeous in velvet or rustling in silk, done up in all the accompaniments of fan, ear-rings, finger-rings, falling sleeves, scent bottle, embroidered bag, hoop and train – all superb, yet all in purest taste . . . a display which no one in these days could accomplish or even fancy'.

Leave the church and rejoin the retaining wall around the Knowe (higher ground). Above you to your left is the gravestone of [11] **SAMUEL GILMORE**, ropemaker, guarded by two grinning skulls separated by a mournful 'winged soul'.

Samuel Gilmore

Walk along the wall beyond the church tower. When you reach the steps on your left go up them following the path as it curves towards the right. To the left are walled tombs, devastated and crumbling, the roofs open to the sky, slabs of stone stacked against flaking walls, pock-marked and peeling like wallpaper.

Now on your right *Memento Mori* catches your eye again under a 'winged soul' with a broken nose. Continue along the path in spite of the unease building up inside you. Knee-high, two hollow-eyed skulls sit at either end of a long leg-bone. Pass carefully round the end of the tombs and up the small incline behind.

Go to the eighth grave against the wall. The headstone has a semi-circular top and tells you that here lies the brilliant English author **[12] THOMAS DE QUINCEY** (1785-1859), the unpredictable 'Opium-Eater'.

Thomas De Quincey

Through the ragged stones and peaty earth of the walled grave behind are the tortured, twisted roots of ancient trees locked round a pointed obelisk, surmounted by the rusted standard of a long-dead gas-lamp. Above it all you see the steeple of St Cuthbert's and its clock with golden hands.

De Quincey was a Manchester boy educated in Bath where, by the age of 15, he became fluent in both Latin and Greek. He was then sent to Manchester Grammar School but ran away to Wales and began a life of wandering the hills, living off his charm and writing business or love-letters for his hosts. He went to London where he fell foul of money-lenders and took to wandering the streets, lonely and penniless. His family helped send him to Oxford University and it was here that he first took opium for toothache. He was to leave Oxford without a degree.

De Quincey admired the poems of Wordsworth and Coleridge and set out to the Lake District to meet them. This he did, even lending Coleridge £300. He returned to London to enter the legal profession but drifted back to the Lake District where he met the muscular literary rogue, John Wilson – known in Edinburgh as 'Christopher North' – the author and editor of *Blackwood's Magazine*.

De Quincey made two visits to Edinburgh with Wilson, the first in 1813. He found refuge in the Debtors' Sanctuary at Holyrood, from which he emerged in the evenings to fascinate the literary men of the city with his racy conversation which sparkled brightest after midnight.

Back in his Lake District cottage, De Quincey continued to take opium – as much as 320 grains a day in 1813. However, he managed to cut down, felt much better and married the 18-year-old daughter of a local farmer.

One year later he was deep into drugs again. This is the period of his life he describes in his *Confessions of an Opium Eater* (1822).

Looking for work and refuge, he settled in Edinburgh in 1828, living at

The metal 'S' which marks the boundary of the Debtors Sanctuary

first with John Wilson in No 8 Gloucester Place, then in Great King Street, then Forres Street, then in Duddingston and finally in No 42 Lothian Street on the site of the present Royal Museum of Scotland in Chambers Street. Kenneth White in his *Travels in the Drifting Dawn* describes his life in the city: 'During his last years De Quincey would roam the nocturnal streets of Edinburgh, a congenial labyrinth, lost in his dreams . . . He had rooms rented all over the old town, transcendental ratholes he would use for working in, cramming them with papers, dossiers, books; till they became "snowed-up" as he put it. At which moment he'd close the door behind him and look for another place. When he died there were several such rooms still rented in his name . . .'

To the left of De Quincey is 'The Amiable American Stranger', **[13] RUFUS WOODWARD** (1793-1823), a graduate of Yale who visited Europe to pursue his studies and restore his health. Instead, he found a picturesque place to die and one of the most original minds as his post-mortem neighbour. His white marble stone is set in an older monument with winged soul and a threatening skull.

Now go back the way you came. Go down the steps towards the church and then make straight for the long wall of graves facing you. Go to the fourth grave from the far left of the wall to the resting-place of **[14] ADAM ROLLAND** (1734-1819) of Gask, Principal Clerk of Session, just touched by the branches of a giant tree.

People used to stop and stare at the

advocate Adam Rolland, who cut an odd figure on Edinburgh's streets. Lord Cockburn described him thus: 'his dresses, which were changed at least twice every day, were always of the same old beau cut. The vicissitudes of fashion being contemptible in the sight of a person who had made up his own mind as to the perfection of a gentleman's outward covering. The favourite hues were black and mulberry; the stuffs – velvet, fine kerseymere and satin. When all got up, no artificial rose could be brighter or stiffer. He was like one of the creatures come to life again in a collection of dried butterflies.'

Walk on to the 24th grave on the wall at your right. It has five Gothic pinnacles set against the sky. Did you glimpse a dark, tall, striking young woman walk past you? It may have been the shadow of the novelist **[15] SUSAN FERRIER** (1782-1854), a very attractive personality whose conversation sparkled with humour and intelligence and whose writing brilliantly captured the small incidents in life and the comedy of humanity.

Susan was the daughter of a lawyer whose friends included Robert Burns and Sir Walter Scott. One of his clients was the Duke of Argyll whose home at Inverary Castle Susan visited a number of times, leaving the narrow world of her home at Churchhill in Morningside.

You too may now leave by the steps up on to Lothian Road, past the newly-restored watchtower.

The Watchtower

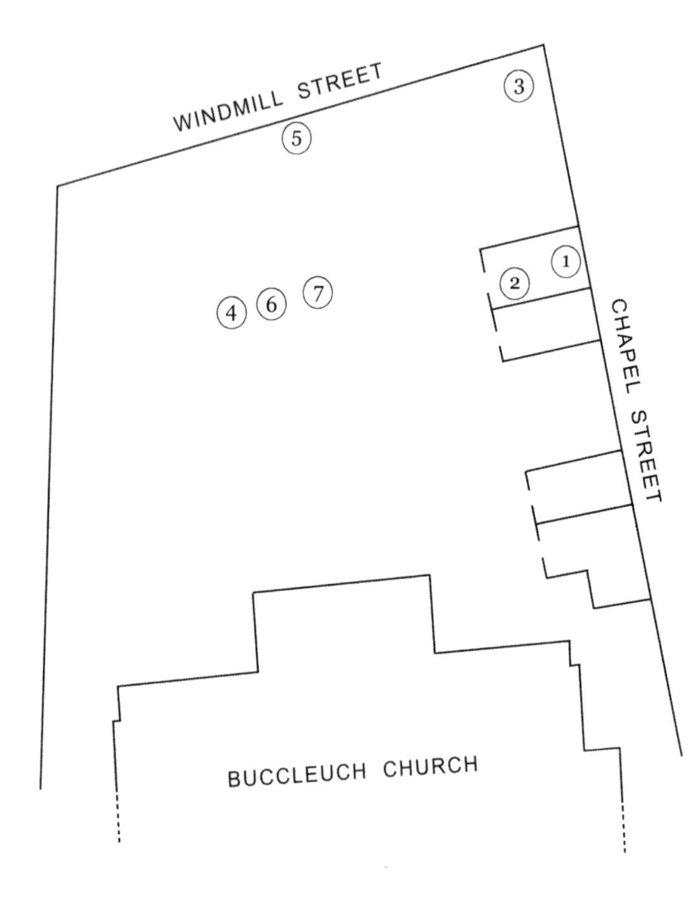

Buccleuch Cemetery

Location – Chapel Street

BUCCLEUCH

Walking south along Potterrow from the Old Town you come to Charles Street. To your right is the little Buccleuch Parish Church (bounded to the north by Windmill Lane), now the property of Edinburgh University and used as a store. Visitors to the cemetery are free to enter during office hours.

Go through the gate and turn hard right. Walk round the side of the church between it and the first walled grave. Keep walking to your right along the wall tombs, heading towards the tower block which dominates the landscape.

Two graves stand together near the far wall. The last is the family grave of **[1]** Dr **ANDREW DUNCAN** (1744-1828), President of the Royal College of Physicians and Professor of the Theory of Medicine at Edinburgh University. Going up two steps you enter the roofless tomb.

Born in St Andrews, Andrew Duncan studied medicine at Edinburgh University before working as a ship's surgeon for the East India Company. He then returned to Edinburgh where he set up practice.

Dr Duncan founded many charitable and useful organisations such as the Royal Public Dispensary, the Caledonian Horticultural Society and the Edinburgh Lunatic Asylum (the latter inspired by the unhappy death of the young poet Robert Fergusson who committed suicide in the then Edinburgh

Bedlam). Dr Duncan is commemorated in the Andrew Duncan Clinic at Morningside.

Dr Duncan's kindness can be seen in the fact that he allowed one of his students to be buried in his own burial-ground. **[2] CHARLES DARWIN** (1758-78) was a member of the celebrated scientific Darwin family: Erasmus Darwin spent a year in 1754 at the Faculty of Medicine in Edinburgh. His three sons (Robert, Francis and Charles) also attended, and both Robert's sons – Erasmus and Charles (the naturalist and author of *The Origin of the Species*), were studying at Edinburgh in 1825. Charles' grandson, Charles Galton Darwin, became Tait Professor of Natural Philosophy at Edinburgh (1923-36).

The obituary of Charles Darwin, Dr Duncan's student, makes it clear that he was exceptionally talented and had been awarded the first medal offered by the Aesculapian Society for developing a criterion to distinguish Matter from Mucus. He had prepared for his final medical examinations on the subject of retrograde motions of the lymphatic vessels.

Walk out of the tomb and continue on to the corner of the wall. Here lies the body of **[3]** Mrs **ALISON RUTHERFORD** (or Cockburn) (1713-94) to whom a plaque on the other side of the wall in Chapel Street is dedicated.

She was a Border lass born near the River Tweed in Selkirkshire. One warm spring morning, while still only a girl, in a green sheltered valley near the Tweed, she heard a soft heart-breaking melody played by a young shepherd on his pipe.

To this music she set her own words, thinking of the recent financial disaster which a number of local lairds had suffered and remembering also the old, sad defeat of the Scottish army in 1513 at the battle of Flodden and the death of the King:

I've seen the forest adorned of the foremost,
With flowers of the fairest, both pleasant and gay;
Full sweet was their blooming, their scent the air perfuming,
But now they are withered, and a' wede away.

Alison Rutherford grew to be a woman of great charm and later married an advocate. In 1786 she met Robert Burns in Edinburgh and wrote: 'The town is at present agog with the ploughman poet, who receives adulation with native dignity and is the very figure of his profession – strong and coarse, but has a most enthusiastic heart of *Love*'.

Her home in Crichton Street was not far from that of Sir Walter Scott, one of her relatives. He tells us 'in her little parlour used to assemble a very distinguished and accomplished circle, among whom [were] David Hume, John Home (the playwright), Lord Monboddo and many other men of name'.

Near this fine old lady in an unmarked grave is buried a man whom Sir Walter Scott labelled 'a determined woman-hater' who always insisted no woman should be present when he came to visit. **[4] DAVID HERD** (1724-1810), collector of Scots songs, lies in an unmarked grave.

Herd was born in Kincardineshire, the son

of a farmer. When he left school he was apprenticed to a country lawyer but soon gave this up and settled in Edinburgh as an accountant's clerk, slaving at copying and book-keeping. His real interest, however, was collecting old books, traditional stories and Scots songs.

In 1769 Herd published 'A Collection of Ancient and Modern Scottish Songs, Heroic Ballads, etc, collected from Memory, Tradition and Ancient Authors'. The *Herd Manuscript* (as it was called) is one of the most authentic collections of ballads and songs. In it Robert Burns found the germ of many of his lyrics.

Sir Walter Scott also acknowledged his debt to Herd. He tells us that Herd 'was known and generally esteemed for his shrewd, manly common sense and antiquarian science, mixed with good nature and great modesty. His hardy, antique mould of countenance and his venerable grizzled locks, procured him, amongst his acquaintance, the name of "Greysteel".'

Herd was a member of the exclusive Cape Club, whose members included Sir Henry Raeburn (the portrait-painter), Deacon Brodie (the burglar) and Robert Fergusson (the poet).

As the echoes of an old Scots tune fade away, they are replaced by a strange unsettling sensation when you move along the wall. Head for the half-way point, between an illegible monument and the grave of **[5]** Dr **ALEXANDER ADAM** (1741-1809), the famous Rector of Edinburgh High School.

Just below the rusty iron cramp high in the wall is the unmarked grave of the notorious **[6]** Deacon **WILLIAM BRODIE**

Dr Jekyll and Mr Hyde

(*d*.1788). Conman and burglar, his two-faced, Janus-like life-style suggested to Robert Louis Stevenson one of his greatest creations – *Dr Jekyll and Mr Hyde*.

In years gone by this was a lonely, shameful spot, marked off by a black iron railing with no memorial, where the once respected and trusted master craftsman and town councillor lay with only the wail of the cold east wind to remember him by.

Brodie was born in the Lawnmarket at Brodie's Close. Like his father, he was a successful cabinet-maker. Robert Louis Stevenson owned one of his chests of drawers and this is now on display in the Writers' Museum.

Brodie rose quickly through the ranks of his craft to become a 'Deacon', a senior official in the Incorporation of Wrights and Masons.

By day he was courteous, respectable, dependable – but by night a different side of his personality emerged. He gambled secretly and lost large sums of money even though he cheated with loaded dice. Then, in 1787 the whole of Edinburgh was baffled by a series of daring and inexplicable burglaries. No one could understand how the thief could have gained entry without leaving a trace.

What no one realised was that William Brodie, using the keys innocently provided for him by his customers, made copies which would then be used for his moonlight activities.

Lantern and keys of Deacon Brodie

At the dead of night Brodie and his gang slipped into the houses they had targeted, stole what they could and then departed as stealthily as they had come. He grew so bold that he actually let himself into a house during the day and walked past an old lady who had lost the power of speech, laughing in her face as he went about his business.

On 5 March 1787 Brodie and his men even tried to rob the Excise House in Chessel's Court. They succeeded but all they got was £16 in shillings and sixpences and a few stamps – they missed £600 hidden in a secret drawer in the cashier's desk!

Not long after, lured by a reward and the promise of a pardon, one of Brodie's

Deacon Brodie

accomplices let the cat out of the bag and revealed just how the robbery had been committed and the identity of the culprits.

Brodie's house was searched. A pair of pistols was found buried underneath the hearth and the other tools of his trade were uncovered – iron wedges, an iron crow-bar, a shaded lantern, false keys and picklocks.

But Brodie was not to be caught so easily. He managed to escape to the Continent and would have sailed off to America but for a careless slip which led to his arrest in a public-house in Amsterdam.

He and one of his accomplices were sentenced to be hanged at the west end of the Luckenbooths (just outside the entrance to St Giles).

As he walked on to the execution-platform, Brodie wore an elegant black suit, his hair was dressed and powdered. After praying with a minister, a white cap was placed on the head of each of the two prisoners and the executioner tied their arms together. Then they found that the noose was on too short a rope. Brodie jumped down and waited patiently while the knots were adjusted. Once again they got up on to the platform but still the rope was incorrectly knotted. Brodie stepped down again.

Finally all was ready. Brodie carefully took off his cravat, opened his shirt collar, buttoned up his waistcoat and coat and helped the executioner to fix the rope. He pulled the white nightcap down over his face and stood with folded arms, waiting.

The watching crowd was immense and suddenly hushed.

His companion dropped his handkerchief as a signal and the table fell away from both of them. The great bell of St Giles tolled as the execution took place. It was a few minutes before 3pm.

Behind him Brodie left the following message: 'My neck now being about to embrace the halter, I would recommend it to all rogues, sharpers, thieves and gamblers whether in high or low station, to take care of theirs, by leaving off their wicked practices and becoming good members of society in future'.

Ironically, the wooden platform and trap-door by which he and his accomplice died had been designed and made by Brodie himself some time previously.

Brodie's Close, in the Lawnmarket

Turn away now with relief. In the centre of the burial-ground, once covered by a church hall and now by red granite chips tastefully railed off, is the unmarked grave of **[7] SUPHY** (Sophia) **JOHNSTON** (1716-1810), one of the most colourful characters in the city.

Suphy was born in Berwickshire. Her father, Robert Johnston of Hilton, was said to have been 'an odd dog'. He decided to bring up his daughter without the discipline of traditional education – she was to be a child of Nature. In fact, he seems to have been an educational pioneer and many of Suphy's quirks of character would be perfectly normal today.

She caused gossip in the neighbourhood when she was seen hunting with her brothers, wrestling with the stable-boys and sawing with the carpenter.

She could shoe a horse quicker than a blacksmith; had learnt how to construct excellent wooden luggage-trunks; played the violin; sang bawdy songs in a bass voice and was a devastatingly accurate mimic.

When she was in her early twenties she persuaded the butler to teach her to read and write.

Suphy Johnston was never well-off, never married but lived to a great age in her flat in Charles Street. Sir Walter Scott, who stayed close by her in George Square, records: 'well do I remember her jockey coat, masculine stride, strong voice and occasional round oath'.

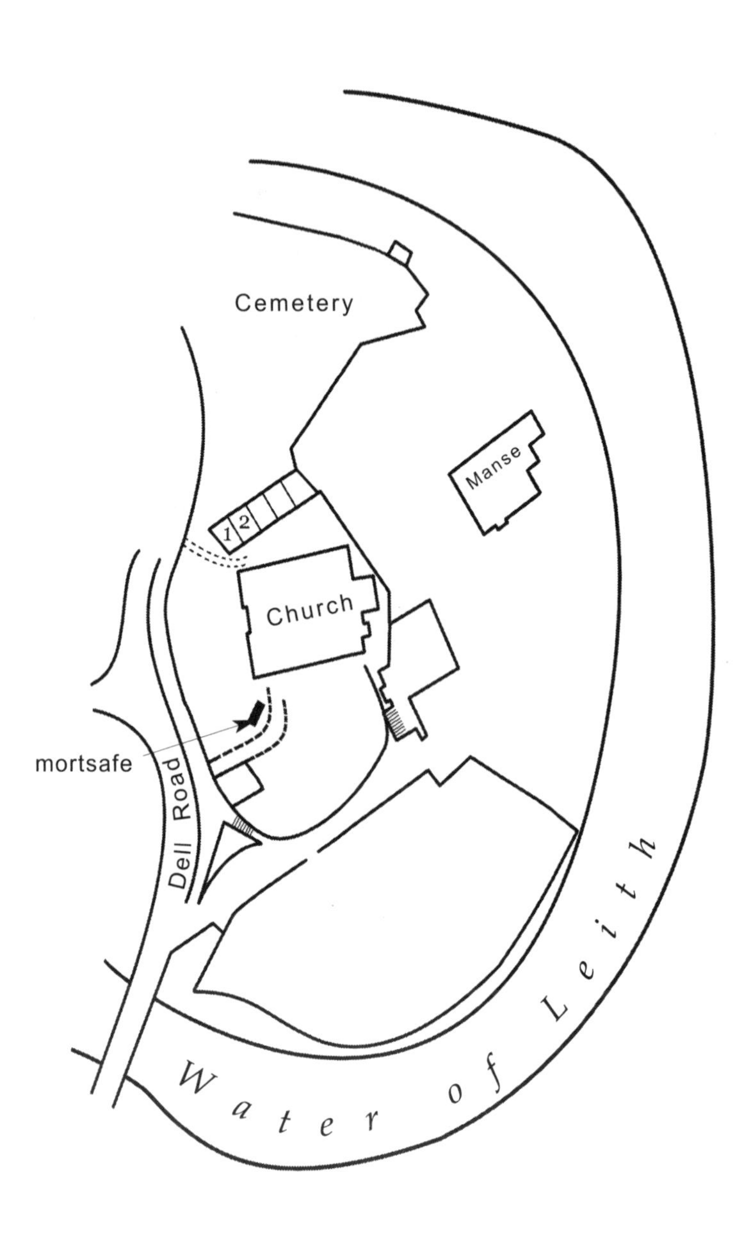

Colinton Churchyard

Location – Dell Road

THE FOLLOWING GRAVEYARDS ARE NOT CENTRAL - A MAP OF THE CITY AREA AND TRANSPORT ARE ADVISABLE

COLINTON

Enter under the arch of the churchyard wall by the iron swing-gate. As you approach the bunched yew trees beside the church, an iron mortsafe (grave security cover) brown with rust crouches at your left like some ancient armoured missile.

Go down the left side of the church until you reach the back of the building.

Perhaps you catch a faint hint of tobacco in the air. As you approach the back of the church a small temple with a pitched roof, barred with a blue iron grill, preserves the mortal remains of **[1] JAMES GILLESPIE** (1725-97), whose illustrious name can also be seen in the mosaic floor encircled by a laurel wreath.

Mortsafe

Shop sign of James Gillespie, tobacconist and snuff-miller

It was down at Spylaw in his snuff-mill that Gillespie worked, an old blanket hanging over his shoulders and a night-cap on his head, like something out of a nursery-rhyme.

His brother John ran their tobacco-shop at No 231 High Street, which was patronised by many of the lawyers and literary figures of the time, including Robert Burns.

Outside the shop stood a wooden black boy holding a clay pipe and leaning on a barrel marked 'Tobacco'. Inside, Gillespie's snuff-grinder worked steadily. Both are in the Museum of Edinburgh (Canongate).

Taking snuff (a form of tobacco) was a popular habit in the 18th century. It might be scented with, for example, orange blossom and would be pinched from a little hollow triangle at the back of the hand, just below the tendon leading into the thumb.

On his death James Gillespie left £12,000 to build a hospital for the elderly and £2,700 to open a free school for poor boys. The

Gillespie's Hospital

hospital was built in Bruntsfield but demolished in 1870 and the income used to provide annual pensions. James Gillespie's School, after a long and honourable history as a fee-paying institution, is now a local authority high school for boys and girls.

Gillespie had a rather prominent nose (as can be seen from the marble bust at the entrance to James Gillespie's High School), and his great commercial success produced the following verse at the sight of his elegant carriage rattling over the cobbles: *Wha wad hae thocht it, That noses had bocht it?*

Walk round to the right side of the Gillespie tomb and you see on the far wall a plaque to the memory of **[2]** Dr **LEWIS BALFOUR** (1777-1860), Robert Louis Stevenson's grandfather and parish minister at Colinton. RLS spent many holidays in his grandfather's large manse, leaving him with many happy memories: 'It was a place in that time like no other . . . the sound of water everywhere, and the sound of mills – the wheel and the dam singing their alternate strain; the birds of every bush and from every corner of the overhanging woods pealing out their notes until the air throbbed with them; and in the midst of this, the manse'. In his verse Stevenson wrote:

Here is the mill with the humming of thunder,
Here is the weir with the wonder of foam.

In the same plot a descendant, **[3]** Lt Commander **DAVID IAN BALFOUR** RN, is buried, killed in action on HMS *Sheffield* during the Falklands conflict of 1982.

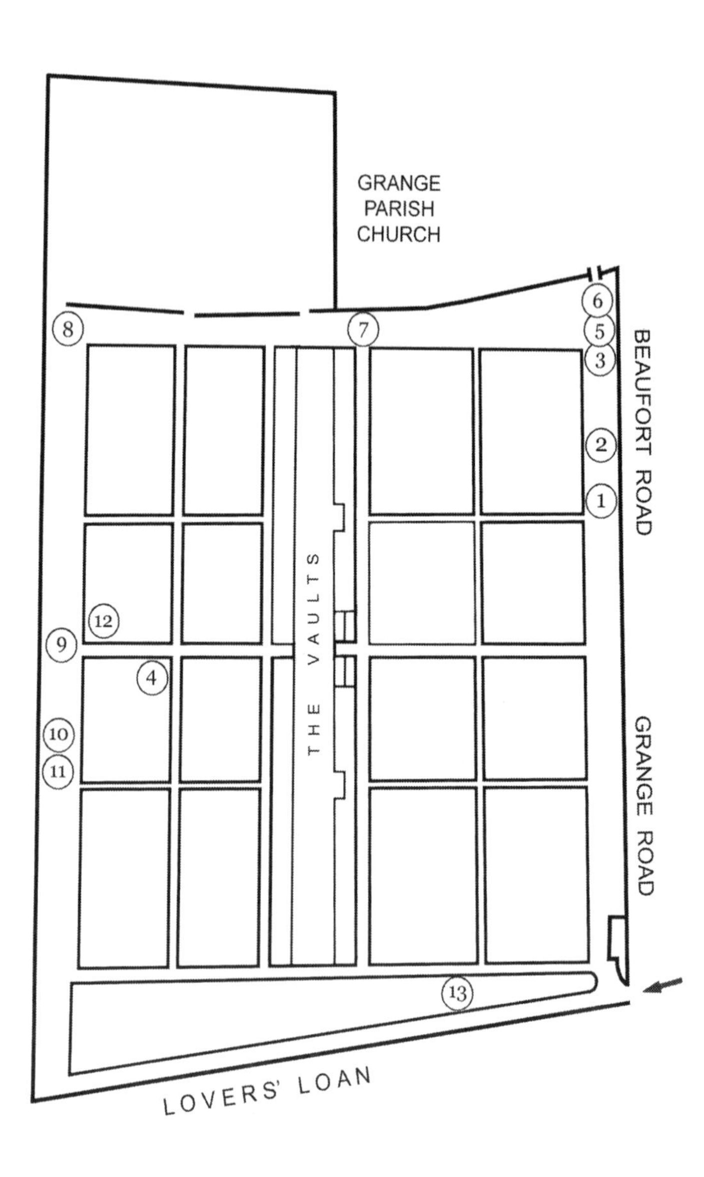

GRANGE CEMETERY

Location – Beaufort Road

GRANGE

Enter the gates of the cemetery from Grange Road opposite the church of St Catherine's-Argyll. To your left outside the gates, beside the narrow Lovers Lane, is a dried-up drinking-fountain set in the wall, a reminder of more leisurely and less sanitary days.

Once you are inside the cemetery turn hard right. Put any idea of ghosts out of your mind. The only unnatural night-time activity here is the mindless vandalism of those who push over headstones for fun in the dark.

Walk along the broad path running beside the north wall which borders Grange Road as it changes into Beaufort Road. First impressions are of a place wide open to the skies, filled with gurgling pigeons – a place of peace.

The sweetness of death

In the depths of a Scottish winter,
William Stuart dreams of warmer shores

Half way along the path look to your right. A mysterious monument – **[1] WILLIAM STUART** – (*d.*1888) calls to you. A half-open door carved from stone under an overhanging palm-tree, heavy with clusters of stone nuts, hints of the unknown.

Pass by this surreal funerary image and nine graves later, on to your right, is the massive memorial to a spiritual giant, the **[2]** Revd **THOMAS CHALMERS** (1780-1847), the Anstruther-born leader of the 'Disruption' in the Church of Scotland.

He was born in Fife, the sixth child of a dyer and shipowner. Even at the age of three he wanted to become a minister. He graduated from St Andrews University and was licensed as a preacher when only 19.

Although he spent some time as a teacher of Mathematics at St Andrews he was ordained a minister in 1803.

Then one day Dr Chalmers had a true conversion experience. His skill as a preacher was transformed and congregations would assemble as much as four hours before a service to hear him.

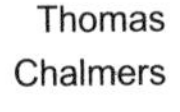

Thomas Chalmers

Lord Cockburn, a close friend, described Dr Chalmers: 'he is awkward and has a low, rough, husky voice, a guttural articulation, a whitish eye and a large dingy countenance. It would not be difficult to find him ugly. But he is saved from this by singular modesty, kindness and simplicity of manner, a strong expression of calm thought and benevolence. The magic lies in the concentrated intensity which agitates every fibre of the man'.

His career as a minister reached a crisis point in 1843 when he and 470 other ministers left the Church of Scotland. They strongly believed that ministers should be appointed by local congregations and not by wealthy patrons as the law of the time demanded. This was the dramatic and painful birth of the Free Church of Scotland.

In 1845 Dr Chalmers became principal of the new Free Church College. But time was not on his side: after Sunday service on 30 May 1847, Dr Chalmers passed away quietly in his bed in Churchhill.

Not much further on, flanked by two grey Celtic crosses, is the large flat monument to Dr Chalmers' great friend **[3] HUGH MILLER** (1802-56), a titanic figure in the worlds of science and religion – a true environmentalist.

Hugh Miller

Born in the magnificent wilderness of Cromarty, Miller spent his childhood soaking up the world around him – the rocks, the sea and a way of life united to the land.

He came to Edinburgh in 1824 to sell a piece of family property but the squalor of the city was a culture-shock. He detested the mean self-interest of those he met while working as a mason on the construction of Niddrie House.

When he returned to Edinburgh it was as the editor of an evangelical Christian paper, *The Witness*. Under his leadership its circulation rose rapidly.

After the Disruption, Miller supported the new Free Church and found an ally in Dr Thomas Chalmers. By the late 1840s Miller had become one of the most respected communicators in Scotland, his most important books being *The Old Red Sandstone* (1841) in which he explained the value of geology, and his autobiography – *My Schools and Schoolmasters* (1854).

But Miller's brilliant mind was also his downfall. Paranoia took the place of genius. There had been a number of violent and unprovoked stranglings at night and he strongly feared that burglars would try to steal the most valuable pieces of his geological collection which he displayed at his Portobello home.

He began to carry a revolver at night for fear of being attacked. He also had a broad dagger and a claymore hidden behind his bed's head-rest. When he began to feel sharp, intermittent stabbing pains inside his head, he became obsessed with the idea that his brain was slowly disintegrating, that he was going mad.

A nightmare prompted him to confide in his doctor: 'I felt as if a sharp knife was suddenly, and as quickly as an electric shock, passed through my brain from front to back'.

Late one evening the maid found him in a fit, his face twisted with horror. But he recovered and spent a happy evening with his family.

Next morning, however, his body was found on the study rug, a hole in his chest made by a bullet from his own revolver. The revolver was found in the bath close beside him. Lying on the table was a sheet of paper with the message: '*Dearest Lydia, my brain burns. I must have walked and a fearful dream rises upon me. I cannot bear the horrible thought. God and the Father of the Lord Jesus Christ have mercy on me . . . farewell.*'

The post-mortem revealed that Miller had been suffering from brain disease.

Further tragedy followed his death, however. The revolver, rusted from lying overnight in Hugh Miller's bath, was taken to the gunsmith who had supplied it, in order to discover exactly how many bullets had been fired. It was lunchtime when the gun was brought into the shop. It was handed over to the foreman **[4] THOMAS LESLIE**, with the words 'Mind, it is loaded'.

Leslie examined the rusty safety-catch. He held it up to his eye. He lifted the hammer to count the bullets. At that instant the pistol went off, blowing his brains out.

Thomas Leslie, who had eight children and had worked with guns for 25 years, was buried in the Grange Cemetery on the very same day as Hugh Miller.

To the left of Hugh Miller's grave is that of **[5] THOMAS NELSON** (1780-1861),

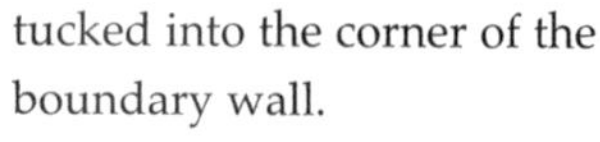

tucked into the corner of the boundary wall.

Nelson founded the publishing firm of Thomas Nelson & Sons which made its name from the re-issue of inexpensive editions of established authors. Next to him lies his son, also **[6] THOMAS NELSON** (1822-92), who worked in the family firm and invented the rotary press in 1850 which made high-speed printing possible.

Return now to the main path and continue along it as it slopes gently up towards Blackford Hill on the horizon behind the trees facing you.

One of the typical features of Victorian cemeteries is the covered vault which runs from side to side of the cemetery, cutting it in two and forming an arresting change of level.

As you reach the road running to your left over the vaults, look right under the gable-end of the church hall at the grey granite stone to **[7] AGNES MURE MACKENZIE** (1891-1955), the Stornoway-born historian and patriot who graduated from Aberdeen University before lecturing in English Literature there and at the University of London's Birkbeck College.

Of all her novels and histories perhaps the best loved were her *History of Scotland* in six volumes and *Scottish Pageant*, her four volume series of Scottish quotations. She was awarded the CBE for her services to Scottish history.

Continue on your way until you reach the end of the wall on your right. The last monument, topped with a triangular pediment, is the grave of **[8] ANDREW USHER** (1826-98), a member of the famous Edinburgh brewing family. You can see his portrait inside the entrance of the Usher Hall, whose construction he made possible in 1896 with a gift of £100,000.

Turn left along the boundary wall and walk on until you meet on your left the central path which runs right through the vaults, cutting the cemetery in two.

Set into the south boundary wall in a place of honour is the last resting-place of **[9]** Dr **THOMAS GUTHRIE** (1803-73), the great social reformer.

Born in Brechin, Guthrie studied surgery and anatomy at Edinburgh University, one of his teachers being the notorious Dr Robert Knox (of Burke and Hare fame).

Further studies brought him to Paris, which opened his eyes to the degrading poverty and the evil of which human beings were capable.

This changed his life for ever and he turned to the Church. He received a licence to preach in 1825 and moved to Forfar as a minister.

When the Disruption came Guthrie was one of the leaders of the Free Church.

Installed at Free St John's in the West Bow in Edinburgh, he began a crusade for a system of 'ragged schools' which would provide shelter, training and education for the many hundreds of children or 'street arabs' who roamed the streets of the capital, learning the lessons of crime and brutality.

Dr Guthrie recorded this interview with one typical urchin: 'Where is your father? *He is dead, sir.* Where is your mother? *Dead too.* Where do you stay? *Sister and I and my little brother live with granny.* What does she do? *Sells sticks, sir.* How do you live? *Go about and get bits of meat, sell matches and sometimes get a trifle from the carriers for running an errand.* Do you go to school? *No.* Have you a bed? *Some straw, sir.'*

Thomas Guthrie

Dr Guthrie was supported in his first 'Plea for Ragged Schools' (1847) by Hugh Miller. In that year three Ragged Schools were set up. Two more 'Pleas' followed in 1849 and 1860 but it was not until 1866 that a new Industrial School Act was finally passed by Parliament.

Walk on along the wall from Dr Guthrie. Eight graves on perhaps you hear a Celtic harp accompanying a man singing the haunting words: *We'll meet and aye be fain, In the land o' the leal.*

Here lie two musicians, father and daughter, one of whose descendants, Nigel Kennedy, has become an internationally-known violinist.

[10] DAVID KENNEDY (1825-86) was the

son of a church *precentor* (leader of singing) in Perth. David developed a rich tenor voice with a wide range and followed his father as precentor in a number of Edinburgh churches, leading the congregation and singing solos.

In 1859 he began his renowned concert career at a Burns centenary concert in Liverpool. This led to long British tours, including appearances in London. Then he and his numerous family travelled worldwide, giving concerts in the USA, Canada, New Zealand, South Africa and India with a repertoire ranging from Handel's 'Messiah' to the 'Auld Scots Sangs'.

Kennedy died of cholera during a concert tour in Stratford, Canada, and his body was brought home to Edinburgh.

[11] MARJORIE KENNEDY-FRASER (1869-1930), was one of his 12 children. Part of her childhood was spent in Perth, although her musical education took place in the Grange district of Edinburgh. From an early age she accompanied her father on the piano and with her brothers and sisters formed a vocal group which toured Scotland.

She accompanied her father on his world tour (1872-76). In Australia they travelled past gum-trees, over hard earth and through locust-storms. She saw the outlaw Ned Kelly, 'caged like a wild beast' in a jail near Melbourne. In New Zealand the family played in sheep-barns illuminated by candles. Next came tours of America and Canada where they travelled by sleigh in temperatures of 20° below zero.

In 1879 another family tour took Marjorie

to South Africa where the floors of their rooms were made of compressed cow-dung washed with milk. They met Edinburgh-born Dr Leander Starr Jameson whose Raid was to start the Boer War.

After vocal training in Italy and Paris, Marjorie returned to Edinburgh in 1882 and began to learn songs in Gaelic.

She married a science teacher, Alec Fraser, in 1887. After he died three years later she set herself up as a music teacher and frequent lecturer on Celtic music.

In 1905 she visted the island of Eriskay, 'an enchanted island'. From here and other Scottish islands she collected melodies and songs, sometimes noting them down by hand, sometimes using a *graphophone* machine to record them.

Her first Hebridean recital came in 1907 and the first of three volumes of *Songs of the Hebrides* was published in 1909. Although her methods are criticised today for changing or adapting folk songs too freely, nevertheless she saved much priceless Gaelic music which, without her, would have disappeared.

Now walk back to the main central path which runs through the vaults. Do you hear a low moaning coming from not too far away? Retrace your steps a few feet passing the grave of Dr Guthrie on your left.

The third large stone monument on your right (opposite that of the nuns of the Ursuline Order at St Margaret's Convent), is that of the unfortunate **[12] ELIZABETH CULLEN CHANTRELLE** (née Dyer) (1851-78), the victim of one of the most heartbreaking murders Edinburgh has ever seen. In death, however, she is not remembered, for although buried in the Dyer family grave, her name does not appear on the stone.

As a young girl of 15 she was sent by her father (a commercial traveller), to the Newington Academy in Arniston Place. There she met Frenchman Eugène Marie Chantrelle, a 43 year old teacher.

Born in Nantes, Chantrelle was the son of a shipowner. He had studied medicine for a short period but during the French Revolution of 1848 his family was bankrupted. He spent some time in America before coming to Scotland. In Edinburgh he rapidly established himself as a skilful teacher of French and Latin.

A romance developed between the charming Chantrelle and his young pupil, Elizabeth Dyer. Then she discovered she was pregnant and, against his will, Chantrelle was forced to marry her. Two months after her wedding, at the age of 16, the first of her four children was born.

But Chantrelle had already grown tired of her. He treated her abominably – swore at her, threatened her and beat her. He went out with other women and flaunted these affairs in her face. Sometimes he locked her out of their home in 51a George Street at night. Many times Elizabeth had to barricade herself from him at her mother's house. Twice she had to call the police in to protect her. After the fourth child had been born she went to see a lawyer about a divorce.

Only love for her children made her stay with Chantrelle. But the beatings continued.

He even threatened her with a pistol.

When his free-spending lifestyle led him into debt, in October 1877 he took out life insurance for £1,000 on his wife. But the policy would only pay him the lump sum if Elizabeth died accidentally. Chantrelle decided on murder, making up an opium mixture with which to poison his wife.

On the morning of 2 January 1878 the maid heard a 'moaning like a cat's' coming from Mrs Chantrelle's room. Three things struck her as strange – the door of the bedroom was slightly open; the gas had gone out (but there was no smell of gas); the baby was no longer in her mother's bed. She noticed green-brown vomit on the bed.

Elizabeth Chantrelle was taken to the Royal Infirmary but died at 4pm.

The police dismissed Chantrelle's claim that a gas leak had accidentally killed his wife especially when eminent witnesses asserted that Chantrelle had fractured the gas-pipe deliberately to draw attention away from the opium which had been found in her vomit.

The Grange Cemetery

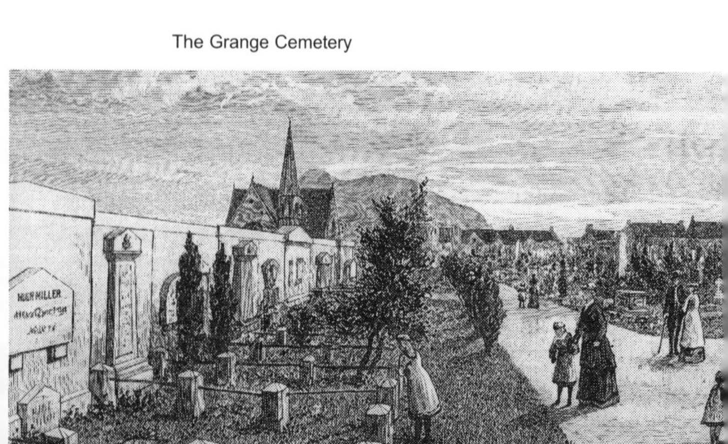

Elizabeth Chantrelle was buried at the Grange in her white wedding-dress, her face calm and unchanged. At the funeral her husband made an embarassing and uncharacteristic outburst of passionate grief. He tried to throw himself into the grave.

Eugène Chantrelle was found guilty of poisoning and hanged on Friday 31 May 1878. The large crowds who came to the Calton Hill were disappointed. The only sign of his execution they saw was the hoisting of the black flag.

Ironically, on the other side of the wall which borders Lovers' Lane is the grave of **[13] MARY JANE PRITCHARD** (neé Taylor) and her mother and father.

Mother of five children, Mary Jane was the victim of the 'Human Crocodile', Dr Edward Pritchard, who poisoned first his mother-in-law with tartarised antimony and then his 38 year old wife Mary Jane in Glasgow.

When his mother-in-law died in Edinburgh, Dr Pritchard callously came through from Glasgow for the funeral.

Later, as his wife lay in her coffin at her parents' home at No 1 Lauder Road, Dr Pritchard made a show of bending down to kiss the lifeless corpse.

But the police eventually became suspicious, exhumed the mother-in-law's body and found it to be full of antimony. Dr Pritchard was arrested and tried at the High Court in Edinburgh. He was found guilty of murder and hanged on 28 July 1895 in Glasgow' Jail square, the last public execution in the city of Glasgow.

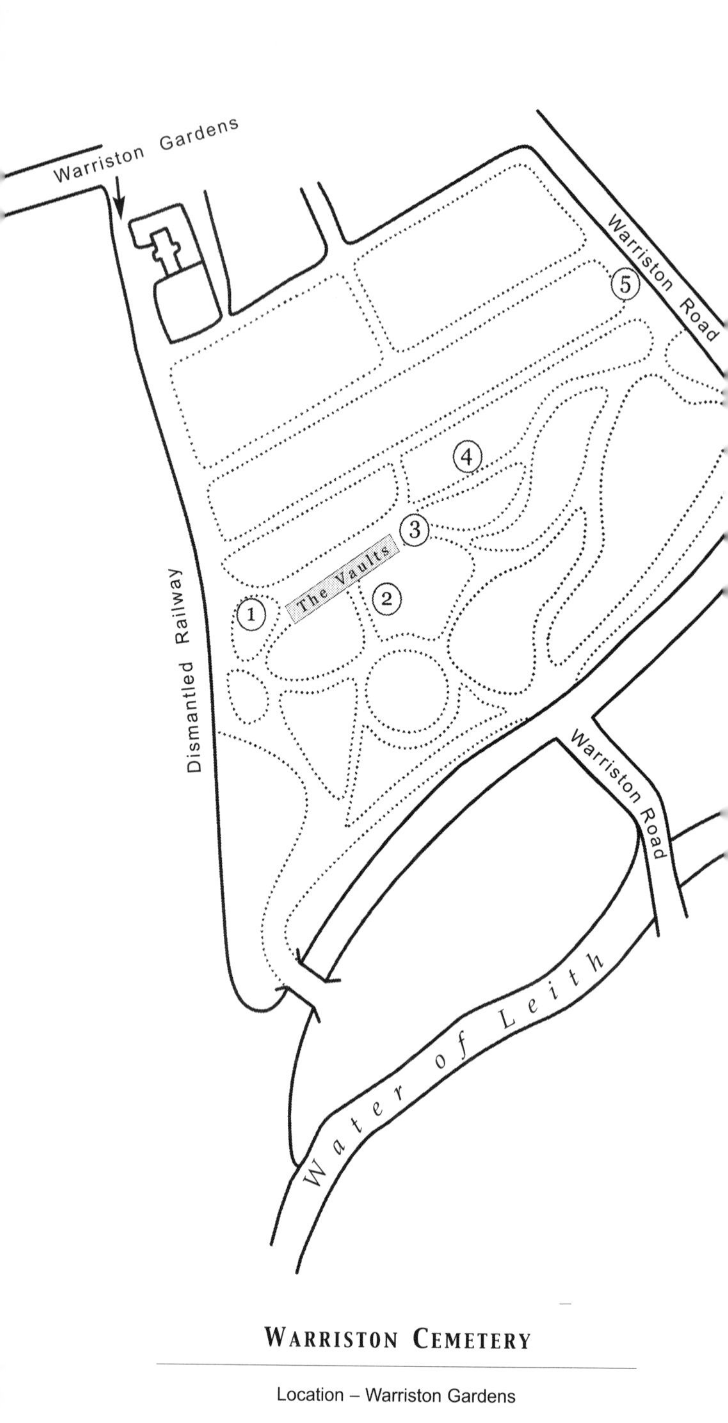

WARRISTON CEMETERY

Location – Warriston Gardens

WARRISTON

There was a time when, for a sharp contrast to the manicured lawns and colourful glass-houses of the Royal Botanic Garden, visitors could turn right off Inverleith Row down to the once aggressive jungles of Warriston Cemetery. For this visit, one church minister advised the intrepid adventurer to wear a pith helmet, bring a sharp machete and carry an elephant-gun! That was before Edinburgh City Council took over the cemetery from the previous management, a private company who had threatened to dig up the burial ground with a view to building a residential estate in its place.

Warriston Cemetery features prominently in Ian Rankin's book, *The Hanging Garden* (1998). His protagonist, Rebus, muses: 'A cemetery should be about death, but Warriston didn't feel that way to Rebus . . . between the tunnel and driveway sat the heart of the place, with its roll-call of Edinburgh's past . . . it had been a history lesson . . . but now he found it a jarring reminder of mortality.'

Go through the blunt stone pillars of the main gate. Walk straight ahead down the path for 143 paces to where the path branches left and right like a wish-bone. Immediately in front of you, as the ground begins to slope down, you come to one of the most pitiful sights in the graveyards of Edinburgh – the tragic remains of the famous 'Red Lady'.

The Red Lady was probably the strangest and most imposing of all Edinburgh's graveside memorials – an arcaded Gothic shrine of white marble with a roof of ruby-coloured glass which bathed with light the figure inside – a sleeping woman **[1] MARY ANN ROBERTSON** (1826-58).

Two small angels once guarded the lintel and praying women stood on the outside wall; there were carved lilies and palms and panes of glass in an Oriental pattern. Inside lay the rosy Sleeping Beauty as pink as if she was in a sauna.

Mary Ann Robertson was the daughter of Brigadier-General Manson of the Bombay Artillery and had married Captain (later General) Alexander Robertson of the 8th King's Regiment.

Her husband became seriously ill with fever at the siege of Delhi in July 1857 and was sent back to his wife. By the following April she had died (whether from the strain of nursing him, history does not record).

The Red Lady as she was

As late as 1984 the Robertson monument still stood, although in some state of disrepair. Today, after an outbreak of mindless vandalism, only the stone foundations remain and a few chips of the ruby glass.

She lies now with her eyes closed, her hands still joined, but her head sliced in two, the lower half of her face smashed open – a white marble figure sunken into a bed of rubble, grass and fleshy weeds.

Follow the path down to the right of the remains of the tomb. The path curves to the left and reaches level ground again. Turn first left along the face of the Gothic vaults which can now be seen on your left.

Not so many years ago (before the City of Edinburgh Council took over Warriston Cemetery), the grey weathered stone of the vaults was smothered in ivy, half hidden behind banks of thistles and fluted pillars of giant hogweed, rusty botanical chandeliers balancing delicate dried florets.

The Red Lady as she is today

John Menzies' basket boy

At the eighth wall monument turn first right and walk 28 paces. On your left is the plain red granite stone marking the grave of **[2] JOHN MENZIES** (1808-79), one of Britain's best-known stationers.

Educated at the Royal High School (where one of his best friends was the inventor James Nasmyth), Menzies served his apprenticeship at an Edinburgh booksellers before working in Fleet Street, London. He returned to Edinburgh in 1833 after his father's death and opened his own shop at the corner of Princes Street and Hanover Street.

Menzies bought up the rights of the works of Charles Dickens and was an agent for *Punch* and *The Scotsman*. Later he opened a network of railway bookstalls, becoming one of the largest booksellers and stationers in the country.

Return to the vaults and continue to the other end where a blocked-up doorway, red spray paint still faintly visible, juts out into the path. The last wall memorial just beyond (a triple one with winged gargoyles), carved from warm orange sandstone is the grave of **[3] ADAM BLACK** (1784-1874), publisher, Liberal MP for Edinburgh and a member of the Town Council.

Black's premises were at the South Bridge and business prospered so that he was able to buy the rights to *The Encyclopaedia Britannica*, to a number of Sir Walter Scott's novels and to involve himself in the publication of *The Edinburgh Review*.

Now you reach a steep slope on your left surmounted by a large obelisk. In front of it is a grassy altar with a retaining wall – this is 'Simpsons' Slope'. With its obelisk and the motto 'Nevertheless I Live', the Simpson family burial ground is where **[4]** Sir **JAMES YOUNG SIMPSON** (1811-70) lies, the pioneer of Anaesthetics.

Simpson's rise to fame came from an undignified collapse under his dining-room table in 52 Queen Street, Edinburgh, on 4 November 1847. Along with some other doctors and assistants, Simpson, by then Professor of Midwifery at Edinburgh, was experimenting with a number of substances which might help to make patients unconscious during medical operations.

After trying bottle after bottle of chemicals he picked up a container with chloroform in it. The doctors present each took a whiff and, in Simpson's words, 'immediately an unwonted hilarity seized the party. They became bright-eyed, very happy and very loquacious. The conversation was of unusual intelligence and quite charmed the listeners. But suddenly there was a talk of sounds being heard like those of a cotton-mill, louder and louder. A moment more, then all was quiet. And then – crash!' So the anaesthetic properties of chloroform were discovered.

Simpson founded the modern practice of Gynaecology and attended Queen Victoria at the birth

James Young Simpson

of Prince Leopold. He was knighted in 1866.

Climb up the slope if you can. When you reach the top, turn right and follow the path as it curves to the left towards the East Entrance of the cemetery. In front of the East Entrance go left to the ninth wall monument. On the wall is a small plaque in memory of **[5] WILLIAM NICOL** (1766-1851), inventor of the Nicol Prism.

Nicol was a geologist, lecturing in Natural Philosophy at Edinburgh University. His prism was made from a rhomb of calcite split and cemented with Canadian balsam. With the prism (known as a 'nicol'), he was able to produce polarised light. This had important applications in Optics and Petrography.

Nicol's other achievements included the making of transparent slivers of stone to be viewed directly through a microscope and a slide-making technique which enabled a large number of fossil woods to be identified.

Warriston Cemetery

PIERSHILL

Coming down the Portobello Road from Jock's Lodge, turn right after Northfield Broadway outside the gates of Piershill Cemetery. Enter and walk 48 paces forward past the white war memorial on your left. From the centre of a grassy mound, a 10-feet white marble stone faces you, towering above the rest of the cemetery. In one corner the stone is signed with a flourish: *'The Great Lafayette'* and on the flat stone below is a dedication – *'In memory of my dearest Beauty'*.

Stand quietly for a moment and feel the drama and excitement generated by this great theatrical performer, a wizard of deception and disguise, a romantic horseman and lion-tamer, a lover and trainer of performing dogs whose astonishing stage-show held audiences spell-bound at the Empire Theatre in Nicolson Street in the spring of 1911. A man whose tragic and violent death stunned the city.

Immensely fit and highly intelligent, the 38-year-old Californian **[1] SIGMUND NEUBURGER**, 'The Great Lafayette', (1873-1911) was a seasoned performer on the circuit of provincial theatres. When at home in London, he

The Great Lafayette

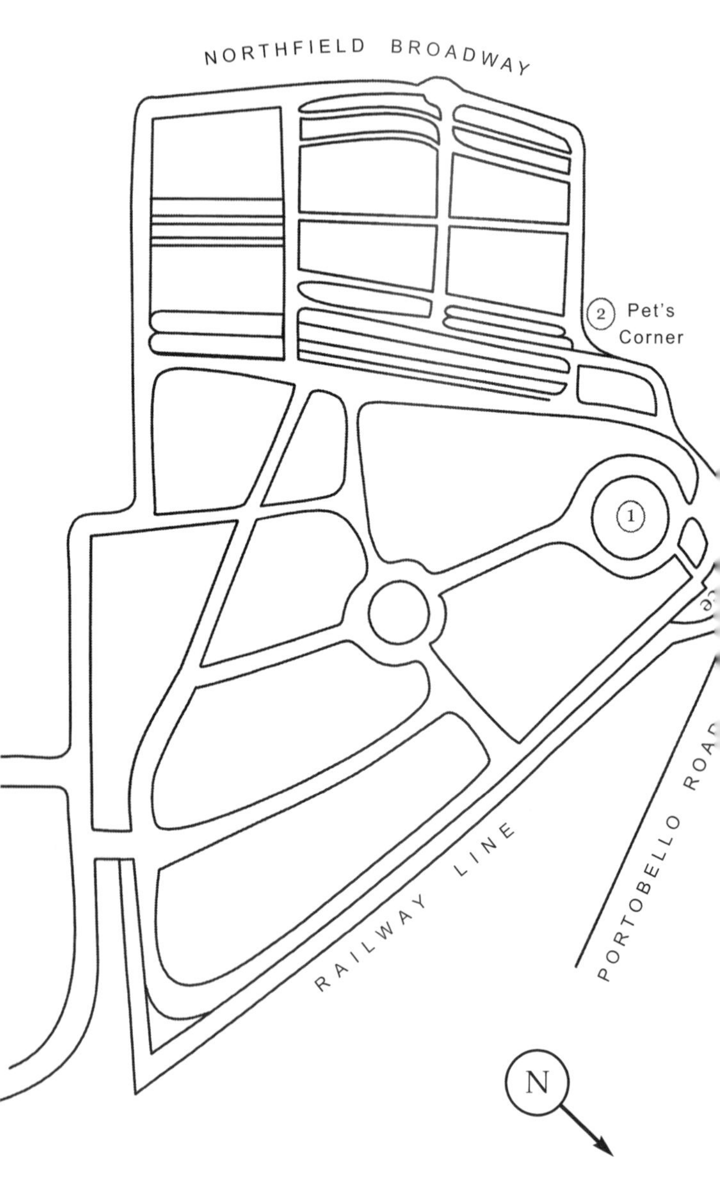

PIERSHILL CEMETERY

Location – Portobello Road

lived in state with his favourite dog 'Beauty', who sat with him at table and whose picture was on his flamboyant cheque-book.

A practising Jew of German extraction (whose father had served as a Captain in the US 13th Cavalry Regiment), he studied fine art but soon turned to the music-hall stage and spent 19 years 'on the road' travelling from one show to the next. His speciality was dramatic illusion carried out under his stage name of 'The Great Lafayette' (named after the French general who defeated Britain during the American Revolution).

In May 1911 Neuburger was into the eighth month of a British tour and had already appeared for a week at the Empire Theatre, Edinburgh, topping the bill. In his second week the 'Man of Mystery' opened with a new feature, thrilling audiences twice-nightly with his dramatic illusion the 'Lion's Bride'.

This was the story of a beautiful Christian maiden, sole survivor of a shipwreck who falls into the hands of an Eastern Pasha (ruler) who puts her in his harem and gives her the choice of loving him or dying in a cage full of lions. She choses the latter.

The maiden is tied hand and feet and, just as she is about to be put into the lion's cage, her true love (The Great Lafayette), arrives on stage riding his black Arab stallion. He fights and kills the Pasha's servant then disappears.

Meanwhile the maiden awaits her terrible fate. Suddenly the lion bounds in and makes straight for her. Just as he is about to pounce he stands up and whips off his head to reveal The Great Lafayette (the real lion having been diverted at the last moment into a side-tunnel).

It was the evening of Tuesday, 11 May 1911. 'The Lion's Bride' was approaching its climax. The theatre was crowded, the stage lavishly draped in exotic Eastern scenery.

Suddenly all the stage-lights 'jumped' as if overloaded with current. An electric wire leading to a lantern fused. A small flame licked up into the scenery and in seconds a large piece hanging above the lantern caught fire. Then the lantern itself toppled into the cushions and draperies on stage. In moments a sheet of flame roared across the footlights, narrowly missing the orchestra. The safety-curtain fell, locking the fire into the backstage area.

The theatre manager rushed down to the conductor of the orchestra shouting 'Play the King!' As 'God Save the King' played, the audience left the theatre in orderly fashion as, behind the curtain, the fire raged out of control. Lafayette ran back across the stage to

The Festival (formerly Empire) Theatre today

search for a member of his company, shouting 'For God's sake, save yourselves!' At that moment, a large beam above the stage collapsed . . .

Within 15 minutes the fire had eaten through the roof of the theatre and a brilliant orange glow lit up the Edinburgh night sky, beneath which shooting flames and white clouds of steam were visible. Inside, the stage was thick with smoke.

Outside, young children in their night-dresses stood beside the performers, their feet covered by the water running from the firemen's hose-pipes. Windows cracked with the heat.

Already the first casualties appeared – a scene shifter badly burned, one of Lafayette's musicians unconscious from the effects of smoke, the theatre's fireman with a badly lacerated hand.

By 3am seven bodies had been found, only four of which could be identified. Of Lafayette there was no sign – and then, finally, a body was found.

The bodies of all the victims were taken to the police mortuary in the Cowgate and identified by the Professor of Forensic Medicine. Afterwards, what was thought to be Lafayette's body was taken to Glasgow and cremated.

Then, in an extraordinary turn of events, the real body of Lafayette was discovered in a hole on the stage and positively identified by the large diamond ring on his right hand and the double gold ring on his left.

The first body thought to be Lafayette had actually been Richards, one of Lafayette's bandsmen, so identical to him in build that Lafayette used him as his double on stage.

Lafayette's real body was taken to the Western Necropolis in Glasgow and cremated.

Ironically, Lafayette's beloved dog 'Beauty', his faithful companion on and off stage for many years and given to him by the illusionist Harry Houdini, had died the previous week and been buried at Piershill Cemetery. Lafayette's ashes were likewise carried to Piershill and laid to rest. Twenty carriages made up the procession as it moved on its way to the cemetery through crowded, silent streets from the funeral parlour in Fountainbridge.

Under a monument of Carrara marble Sigmund Neuburger was laid to rest, as he had requested only a few days before – beside his inseparable 'Beauty'. Among the many floral tributes was one from Houdini.

Some months later rumours filtered back to Edinburgh of a new 'Lion's Bride' illusion being performed in America. But when the

Funeral of the Great Lafayette

Captain Davies

climax came the actor in the lion's skin did not lift off his mask. Had 'The Great Lafayette' performed the greatest illusion of all and survived the flames?

Today, the improved and upgraded Empire Theatre, now known as the Edinburgh Festival Theatre, offers talks and backstage tours on the history of the theatre, including the tragic story of 'The Great Lafayette'.

Stand with your back to the memorial and look to your left towards Arthur's Seat. Walk down in that direction towards for 60 paces to the tiny Pets' Cemetery divided off by a red brick wall.

In the enclosure, note the striking grave of the **[2]** Alsatian **'CAPTAIN DAVIES'** (1957-67), a pillar of polished red granite with the bronze head of an Alsatian dog on top, shaded by two evergreen trees. It is only one of the hundreds of memorials to pet dogs, cats and cage birds.

As you leave and come down from the mound, look across the road to see the massive Craigentinny Marbles towering above the bungalows.

Rosebank Cemetery

Location – Pilrig Street

ROSEBANK

Enter by Pilrig Street and head towards the massive weeping tree just inside the entrance. Turn first right along the path and follow it beside the wall for 94 paces. Follow the path as it turns sharp left and carry on for another 60 paces until you are opposite the brown harled gable-end of the tenement block over the wall. Walk 30 paces towards it to a white marble stone set into the wall.

Towards the end of the 19th century an old man in a black coat could be seen most days in Princes Street Gardens feeding the birds in the shadow of the Scott Monument. He was **[1] ANDREW YOUNG** (1807-89), a retired headmaster and composer of the well-known hymn 'There is a Happy Land'.

Also in Princes Street Gardens, near the National Gallery, the huge dark statue of John Wilson stands with his head in the trees. He taught Andrew Young at Edinburgh University and awarded him a prize for writing a poem on the Scottish Highlands. Young went on to become Headmaster of Niddry Street School.

While on holiday in Rothesay in 1828 Young heard his hostess, a Mrs Marshall, play an Indian tune – 'The Battle March of Delhi' – on the piano. He called out to her to 'play it once again, please. The tune will appeal to my young folks in Niddry Street.' He left the house humming the tune, which haunted him right through the night.

Walking in the garden next morning he set words to the music and so created a hymn which was to be translated into more than 30 languages:

There is a happy land,
Far, far away,
Where Saints in glory stand,
Bright, bright as day.

After retiring as headmaster of Madras College, St Andrews, Young died at 22 Elm Row, Edinburgh, on St Andrew's Day 1889.

Continue along the grass skirting the wall. Pass a locked gate and head for the corner. Just before you reach it, under a bus-stop, is a large wall-monument and a Celtic cross swollen with bulging knots while the lion rampant of Scotland claws the air. This is the 'Field of Coffins', the tragic remains of Britain's worst rail disaster, an event which led to 227 deaths and stunned the nation.

On that terrible day of 22 May 1915, the enthusiastic volunteers of the **[2] ROYAL SCOTS**, 7th Leith Battalion (Territorials) set out from Larbert bound, via Liverpool, for the

The Quintinshill Disaster

Dardanelles and Gallipoli. There were 500 men of the regiment on board as the train, travelling at 50 miles an hour, neared Quintinshill signal box just outside Gretna.

Just after 6.30am the troop carrier with 16 officers and 470 men of the Royal Scots exploded head-first into a 120 ton local train. The first three coaches of the troop train fragmented instantly. Three minutes later the Euston to Glasgow express roared into the wreckage, bulldozing the troop train over a nearby goods train.

For a brief moment there was a dreadful silence. Then fire broke out and screams were heard over the hiss of escaping hot water and steam. The steel frames of the carriages became white-hot. Bullets and gas-cylinders exploded.

Those less injured struggled to rescue their comrades and the passengers from the Euston express. Doctors were forced to amputate with carpenters' saws, cutting off limbs in less than 30 seconds.

In Leith's Dalmeny Street drill hall, row upon row of coffins were laid out. At the public funeral ceremony, thousands lined Pilrig Street. As the procession passed the 'Dead March from *Saul*' was played, three volleys were fired and, in the interval between each, a pipe-major of the 3rd Royal Scots played a stave of 'Lochaber No More'. The ceremony ended with 'The Last Post'.

At the graveside monument are the lines:

Yea, though I walk through the valley of
the shadow of Death, I will fear no evil:
for Thou art with me.

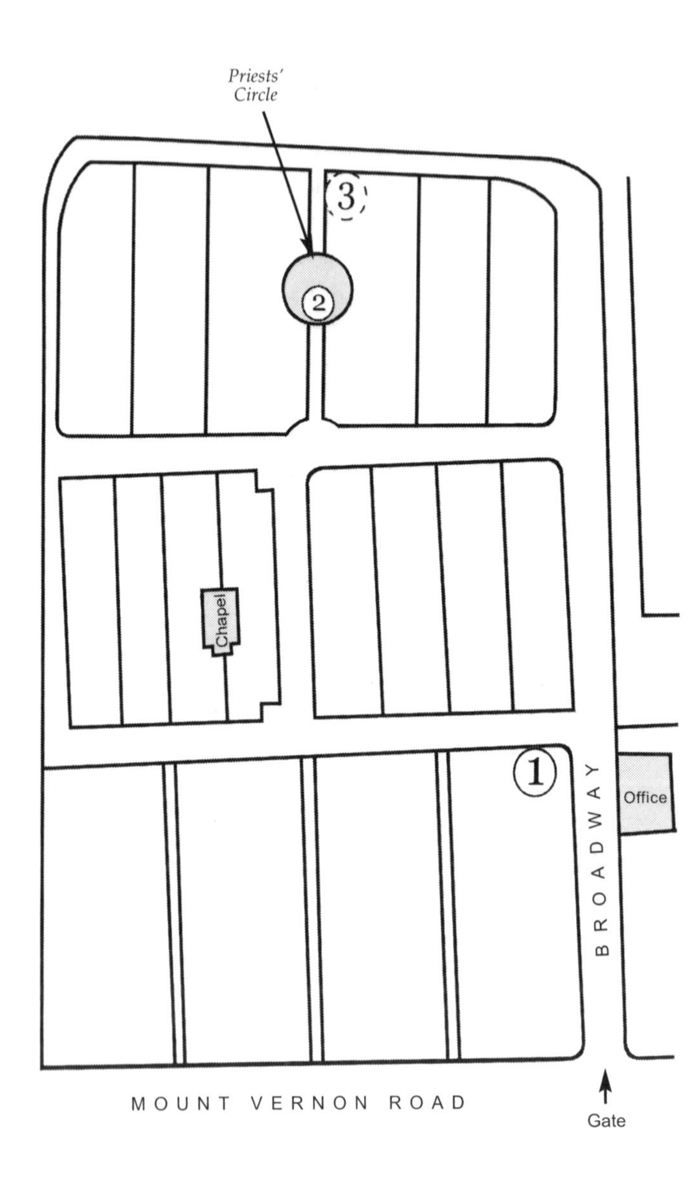

Mount Vernon Cemetery

Location – Mount Vernon Road

Mount Vernon

Enter by the black iron gates past a weeping willow and the cemetery offices. Take the first turning to the left and walk towards the tall Monkey Puzzle tree. After 30 paces stop at the 11th gravestone to your left, a simple polished grey granite stone with a small Celtic cross engraved above the inscription.

[1] TOM MACDONALD (Tómas Dubhghlas MacDòmhnaill – aka *Fionn MacColla* (1906-75) was brought up in Montrose as a Plymouth Brother. In time, he rejected the contemporary narrowness of the Scottish religious outlook and turned instead to the Gaelic past.

'Had the community retained,' wrote MacColla, 'as it had in Gaelic, a language of immense strength and resources potentially equal to any other, and of unsurpassed mellifluence then the community of Albannaich instead of falling to the condition of "the greatest cultural desert in Europe", would necessarily have developed into a veritable oasis of unexcelled fertility and of vast extent in the area of the human spirit.'

Go forward again. Turn first right, passing the small chapel and walk towards the far-off black-topped chimneys and tower-blocks. Behind you are the magnificent slopes of Arthur's Seat. To your left Craigmillar Castle emerges out of a green wooded hill.

At the T-junction, skirt round the semi-circular plot and continue on in the same direction towards the far wall. You reach a circle at the heart of the cemetery – the *Priests' Circle* surrounded by small white engraved stones.

Here, in an unmarked grave, lies **[2]** Canon **JOHN GRAY** (1816-1934), a London man who became a Roman Catholic, studied at the Scots College in Rome and was ordained a priest in 1901.

He was appointed first as a curate in Edinburgh's Cowgate and in 1906 was sent to St Peter's in Morningside, a church designed for Gray by Sir Robert Lorimer and largely funded by an emigré Russian, André Raffalovitch (who is buried nearby), a man of fine artistic taste and a friend of the decadent satirical artist Aubrey Beardsley.

Raffalovitch was responsible for Canon Gray's conversion. He held the last regular literary salon in Edinburgh on the grand 19th-century scale. They had literature in common as Canon Gray had, in his youth, been a minor poet associated with Oscar Wilde.

Go past the life-sized granite crucifix and walk towards the boundary wall. Here, until very recently, in the last grave on your right (decorated with white marble pots full of

Margaret Sinclair

bright flowers trembling in the breeze and with three wide marble steps) was formerly the grave of the dustman's daughter, **[3]** the Venerable **MARGARET SINCLAIR** (1900-25).

Margaret Sinclair lived in the Cowgate, at that time one of the poorest parts of the city just below the High Street. As a young girl she worked hard and studied for certificates in dress-making, cooking and sewing, all of which were intended to help her find a job as a house-maid.

To support her family, she worked part-time as a commercial messenger before taking up a full-time job as a French polisher, becoming an active trade union member.

When the Waverley Cabinet Works closed in 1918 she found a job at McVitie's Biscuit Factory. But another calling came to her. She thought long and hard about her life and then became a nun, joining the Order of Poor Clares in a London convent.

There she died, suffering from incurable tuberculosis. After her death miraculous cures were reported by many who prayed in her name. Today, Margaret Sinclair is commonly referred to as the 'Edinburgh Wonder Worker' and in 1978 was declared Venerable by the Roman Catholic Church, an important step towards canonisation.

Two years after her death Margaret's body was exhumed from Kensal Green Cemetery, London and re-interred at Mount Vernon in Edinburgh. On 6 October 2003 her body and its monument were taken to a new place of rest at a side-chapel in St Patrick's church in the Cowgate.

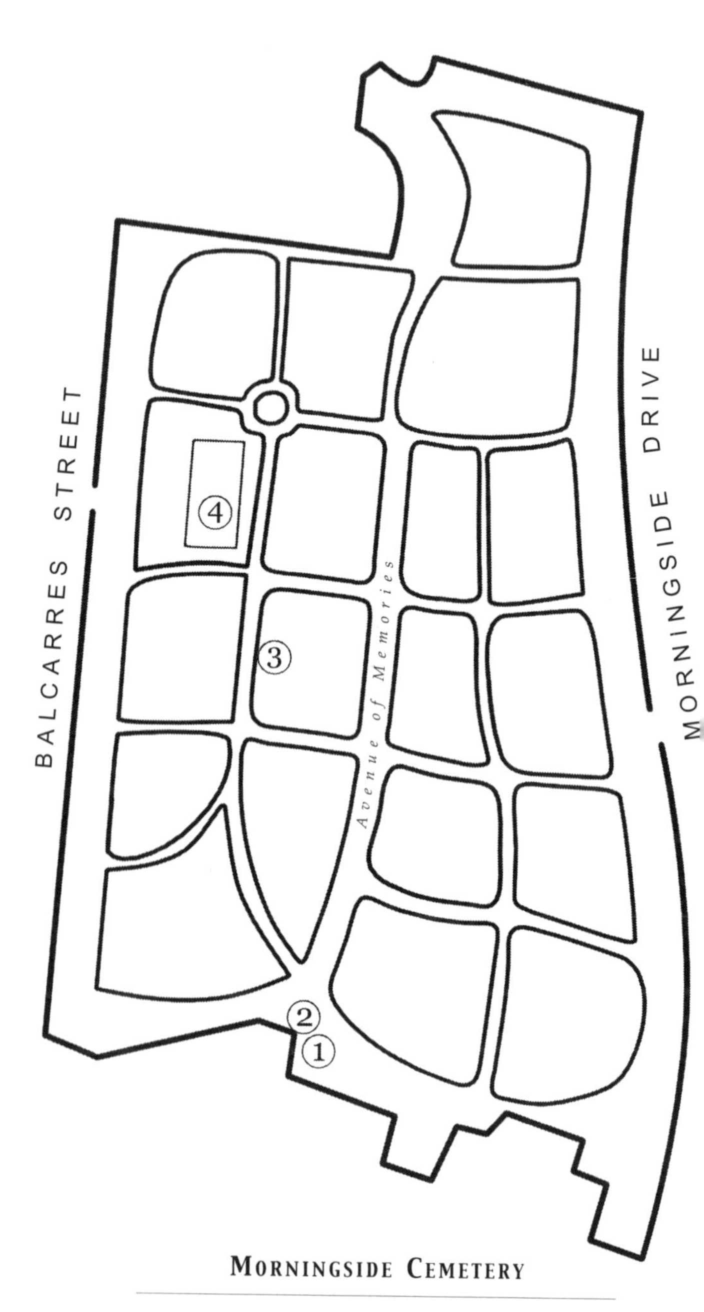

MORNINGSIDE CEMETERY

Location – Morningside Drive

Morningside

Enter off Morningside Drive (just past Ethel Terrace). Turn first left and follow the path round the perimeter for 250 paces as it slowly curves right. Stop at the first of a group of four clean grey, rough-hewn granite headstones.

Edinburgh University has had several Nobel Prizewinners on its staff, including Charles Glover Barkla, Professor of Natural Philosophy 1913-22 (whose award was for showing the nature of X-radiation) and Max Born (quantum mechanics, 1954).

Professor **[1]** Sir **EDWARD APPLETON** (1892-1965) was a Bradford boy who studied at Cambridge under Lord Rutherford before serving during the First World War in the Royal Engineers. Later he returned to Cambridge to conduct research into radio waves. In 1924, he became Professor of Physics at London University and in 1936 Professor of Natural Philosophy at Cambridge.

In 1924 he discovered a layer in the atmosphere which was named the Appleton Layer in his honour. His work was crucial in the development of radar which would have a decisive influence on the outcome of the Battle of Britain.

In 1941 Appleton was put in charge of all British work on the atom bomb and his research into the Ionosphere made ionospheric forecasts possible.

Edward Appleton

George Lichtenstein

He was awarded the Nobel Prize for Physics in 1947 and became Principal and Vice-Chancellor of the University of Edinburgh, 1948-65.

Fourteen paces further on, with its back to you, is a blunt grey obelisk. Can you hear the gentle notes of a piano in the distance? Walk round the obelisk. There is a seven-stringed lyre carved into the stone and an inscription in Hungarian.

[2] GEORGE LICHTENSTEIN (1827-93) was born in Szigetvár, Hungary, and settled in Edinburgh, making his first appearance as a pianist at the Theatre Royal. Probably his most memorable concert was when he played Schumann's 'Andante with Variations for two pianofortes' in the Hopetoun Rooms in Queen Street with Madame Schumann.

But Lichtenstein had lived through even sterner tests. At the Prussian Court, he had been the representative of the Provisional Government of the Hungarian revolutionary leader Lajos Kossuth. In 1849, as private secretary to Kossuth, he was actually on the bridge between Buda and Pest when the Plenipotentiary sent from Vienna to close the Hungarian Parliament was dragged from his carriage and murdered. Kossuth, it was reported, folded his arms and said 'My poor country, you will pay dearly for this.'

In the war with Austria which followed George Lichtenstein lived in great danger and long afterwards carried in his despatch-box the noose which he would have had to use if the Austrians had known what he was really up to. Kossuth's independent Hungarian republic was eventually destroyed by Russia in August 1849.

Lichtenstein was one of the most famous music teachers in Edinburgh and a founder of the Edinburgh Society of Musicians. When the future Edward VII was sent to Holyroodhouse to study at the Royal High School nearby, Lichtenstein was chosen to accompany his playing on the violin.

Now walk forward down the slope under the Monkey Puzzle tree towards the far boundary wall of the cemetery. When the ground levels out you will see in the distance the tall white First World War memorial cross between two weeping trees. Go towards it.

After 65 paces you find yourself beside a red sandstone wayside shrine on your right to **[3] MARY McCULLOGH** (1854-85). In its weathered alcove stands a woman in white leaning on a rough stone cross, one hand on her heart.

Through the trees you suddenly hear a starting-pistol followed by bursts of cheering. You might see a figure in white running-shorts powering over the cinders.

Mary McCulloch

Walk forward 40 paces. To your left is a wild holly tree. Beside it is the 30-metre square paupers' grave raised above the level of the path. Here lies **[4] ALFRED REYNOLDS DOWNER** (1873-1912). Downer was born in Jamaica but his parents were from the Borders and he was brought up and educated in Edinburgh, first at George Watson's and then at Melville College.

While living in Glasgow in 1890, Downer's first senior races were for Clydesdale Harriers. Over the next two years he steadily improved his times, winning races in Edinburgh at Myreside, Warriston and Tynecastle.

He broke the Scottish 120 yards record twice in 1893 in the space of a month, and at a meeting in Glasgow he won the 100, 220 and 440 yards, in spite of stumbling and almost falling at the start of the quarter mile. This day of achievement was known as 'Downer's Day'.

Some months later Downer was

Alfred R. Downer

charged with having asked for payment from certain clubs and was suspended by the Scottish Amateur Athletic Association. Other athletes, however, were also involved including Rangers Football Club whose good influences saved the day for Downer and his suspension was lifted.

Downer turned professional in 1896 and reached the summit of his career over the next two years. He ran the fastest time off the mark in the 130 yards handicap at Powderhall (which he won in a time of $13^{2}/_{5}$ seconds and the following year was unquestionably the fastest short-distance runner in the world, nicknamed 'The Flying Scotsman'.

Some time later, while competing in a meeting in Paris, he had a bad fall in a hurdle race. He returned home to Edinburgh with an injured tendon, thoroughly exhausted.

His running days were over. He went into business but his health never recovered. Racked by syphilis, Downer died in poverty at the Morningside Asylum.

Morningside Cemetery, with Arthur's Seat in the background

RESTALRIG

Location – South Restalrig Road

The memorial stone of **[1] LOUIS CAUVIN** faces the main door of St Margaret's Church, Restalrig. It is set into the wall of the medieval St Triduana's Well, celebrated for its therapeutic waters which healed eye diseases.

Cauvin was born in the parish of South Leith, son of an exiled Frenchman and a Scotswoman. Cauvin's father was a tenant farmer but was also well-known for giving French lessons.

Educated at the High School, the College (University) of Edinburgh and the University of Paris, Louis followed his father into teaching, working from eight in the morning to nine at night, impressing all his pupils with his infectious enthusiasm and discipline. In his High Street premises, he taught Robert Burns three times a week for three months during 1786-87; the lessons starting at 9pm, after Cauvin's normal teaching day was over.

Elegantly dressed and generous to those less fortunate than himself, Cauvin ended his life a wealthy man, leaving his fortune for the construction of a residential school for the orphan children of teachers, farmers and booksellers. This ultimately became the Dean Orphanage at Belford Road – today the National Galleries of Scotland's Dean Gallery (which, appropriately enough, houses not only the Paolozzi Archive but the Keiller Surrealist collection with its echoes of France).

CRAIGENTINNY

Location – Craigentinny Crescent

Down Portobello Road and opposite the entrance to Piershill Cemetery is the road to Craigentinny Crescent. Take the second turning on the left up Craigentinny Crescent.

One hundred yards on the left is the extraordinary Craigentinny Marbles (Edinburgh's version of the Elgin Marbles) flaunting a Babylonian procession with oxen, camels and dancing women shaking tambourines as Pharoah and his army of chariots and horses falls into the sea. White seagulls sit unmoved on the roof. Lions guard the eaves. Masses of carved flowers hang heavily in swags.

William Henry Miller

The Craigentinny Marbles

This is the awesome grave of **[1] WILLIAM HENRY MILLER** (1789-1848) and all this glory was a result of the Millers being one of the leading Quaker families in Edinburgh at that time – his grandfather was market-gardener to Holyrood Palace.

Born in Paris, Miller graduated from the University of Cambridge to become Tory MP for Newcastle-under-Lyme (1830-41). He was also a scholar and a collector of fine books, whose library of early English literature was of exceptional quality.

A secretive, reclusive man, he had a reputation for being eccentric and his last days were spent in seclusion at Craigentinny House, the family home.

His magnificent mausoleum, based on the Temple of Vesta at Tivoli, was constructed in what was once the garden of Craigentinny House.

TRON KIRK

Location – High Street

When **[1] WALTER MERLIOUN** (1465-*c.*1550) died, his last wish was to be buried in the middle of the High Street, which he and his brother had constructed. He wanted the people of his adopted city to walk all over him – to be 'in with the bricks'.

Merlioun (corrupted to 'Marlin'), and his brother John were French master masons who settled in Edinburgh having been brought north to introduce Continental construction techniques.

On 20 June 1499 James IV granted a pension to Walter Merlioun to keep him in Scotland. In return, Merlioun built the two-storey vaulted pend of the Holyrood Gatehouse in 1502. Today it is walled up but can still be seen.

Merlioun is best known as the supervisor of the construction of the cambered stone surface of the High Street which, with his craftsmen John and Bartoulmé Foliot, he installed in 1532.

This 'causey' (causeway) produced a number of Scots expressions such as 'to keep the crown of the causey' (to appear openly without having to lurk or go down obscure alleys). The function of the sloping sides of

'The Heart of Midlothian', High Street

the paved street was to keep the surface of the road dry by allowing water to drain off efficiently.

Merlioun was a man of standing in Edinburgh. He owned land in the Cowgate and even became a burgess. In 1540 his brother John built the Register House at Edinburgh Castle.

After he died, Merlioun's grave at the top of Marlin's Wynd was marked by six flat stones. When the Tron Kirk was built over Marlin's Wynd (1736-47), the grave of Walter Merlioun was forgotten and some of the six sculptured stones built into Portobello Tower (1785). In 1974 renovations to the interior of the Tron Kirk allowed archaeologists to excavate the ground around the foundations. Underneath was discovered the original cobbled roadway of Marlin's Wynd.

Marlin's Wynd

APPENDIX

The Edinburgh burial grounds, churchyards and cemeteries listed immediately below are the responsibility of the Department of Environmental and Consumer Services. In most cases Historic Scotland also has a key role in conserving historic gravestones.

Old Calton Burial Ground (Waterloo Place); New Calton Burial Ground (Regent Road); Canongate Churchyard (Canongate); Colinton Churchyard (Spylaw Road); Corstorphine Hill Cemetery (Drum Brae South / North); Cramond Churchyard (The Glebe); Currie Churchyard (Currie Village); Dalry Cemetery (Dalry Road); Duddingston Churchyard (Duddingston Village); Grange Cemetery (Beaufort Road); Greyfriars Churchyard (Candlemaker Row); North Leith Churchyard (Coburg Street); Liberton Cemetery (Liberton Brae); Morningside Cemetery (Morningside Drive); Mortonhall Cemetery (Howdenhall Road); Newington Cemetery (Dalkeith Road); North Merchiston Cemetery (Slateford Road); Portobello Cemetery (Milton Road East); St Margaret's (Restalrig); East Preston Street Cemetery (East Preston Street); Dalmeny Churchyard (Dalmeny Village); Jewish Cemetery (Braid Road).

Other cemeteries and graveyards are privately or nationally owned: Edinburgh Castle; the Palace of Holyroodhouse; St John the Evangelist; St Cuthbert's; The Dean Cemetery; Buccleuch Church; Mount Vernon; Piershill.

USEFUL ADDRESSES

Carved Stones Adviser Project (Council for Scottish Archaeology, supported by Historic Scotland), www.scottishgraveyards.org.uk

Department of Environmental and Consumer Services, City of Edinburgh Council at Mortonhall Crematorium, Howdenhall Road (tel: 0131 664 4314, www.edinburgh.gov.uk).

Exhibition of the History of Surgery
Royal College of Surgeons, 9 Hill Square, Edinburgh, EH8 9DR, tel: +44 (0)131 527 1600 www.rcsed.ac.uk

Historic Scotland, Longmore House, Salisbury Place, Edinburgh, EH9 1SH, tel +44 (0)131 668 8600, www.historic-scotland.gov.uk

Royal College of Physicians
9 Queen Street, Edinburgh, EH2 1JQ
tel: +44 (0)131 225 7324, www.rcpe.ac.uk

Royal Commission on the Ancient and Historical Monuments of Scotland, 16 Bernard Terrace, Edinburgh, EH8 9NX
tel: +44 (0)131 662 1456, www.rcahms.gov.uk

Scottish Archive Network: project whose partners are the National Archives of Scotland (NAS), the Heritage Lottery Fund (HLF) and the Genealogical Society of Utah (GSU)
www.scan.org.uk

VisitScotland (Scottish Tourist Board),
23 Ravelston Terrace, Edinburgh, EH4 3TP
tel: +44 (0)845 22 55 121,
www.visitscotland.com

ACKNOWLEDGEMENTS

The author and publisher gratefully thank the following for their help and permissions:

Kenneth White, *Travels in the Drifting Dawn* (Mainstream Publishing, Edinburgh, 1989) and Ian Rankin, *The Hanging Garden* (Orion Books Ltd., London, 1999).

Also thanks to Archie Foley, Frank Hanlon, Fr Ed Hone (St Patrick's Church), Historic Scotland, the Royal Commission on the Ancient and Historic Monuments of Scotland, Dean Cemetery Trust, St Giles High Kirk, the Faculty of Advocates, the Royal College of Surgeons of Edinburgh, the Signet Library, the Royal College of Physicans of Edinburgh, the Royal Scots Dragoon Guards, Edinburgh Festival Theatre and the City of Edinburgh Council.

Every reasonable effort has been made (unsuccessfully) to trace the holder of the copyright to photographs published in 1925 by Francis Caird Inglis.

SELECTED READING

Anderson, P. A., *Silences that Speak* (Alex Brunton, Edinburgh, 1931)

Boyle, A., and C. Dickson, A. McEwan, C. Maclean, *Edinburgh's Neglected Heritage* (History of Science Unit, Edinburgh, 1985)

Robinson, George, *Edinburgh Castle's Dog Cemetery* (Cowan Print, Edinburgh, 2004)

Willsher, Betty and Edwina Proudfoot (eds.), *Understanding Scottish Graveyards* (Canongate Books, Edinburgh, 1995)

INDEX

The name of the person is followed by their burial ground (in brackets): **(B)** Buccleuch; **(C)** Colinton; **(CG)** Canongate; **(CT)** Craigentinny; **(D)** Dean; **(EC)** Edinburgh Castle; **(G)** Grange; **(GF)** Greyfriars; **(H)** Holyrood Abbey; **(M)** Morningside; **(MV)** Mount Vernon; **(NC)** New Calton; **(OC)** Old Calton; **(P)** Piershill; **(R)** Restalrig; **(RB)** Rosebank; **(SC)** St Cuthbert's; **(SG)** St Giles; **(SJ)** St John's; **(TK)** Tron Kirk; **(W)** Warriston